AN UNDERSTANDING OF ALBERT SCHWEITZER

An Understanding of ALBERT SCHWEITZER

by

George N. Marshall

PHILOSOPHICAL LIBRARY
New York

Published, 1966, by Philosophical Library, Inc.
15 East 40th Street, New York 16, N.Y.

Library of Congress Catalog Card No. 65-28763

Printed in the United States of America

To

My Wife and Son

Barbara Ambrose Marshall
Charles Hopkinson Marshall

IN MEMORIAM
ALBERT SCHWEITZER, 1875-1965

and to

Older comrades who inspired my quest for an understanding and personal knowledge of Dr. Schweitzer

Dean Clarence Russell Skinner, 1881-1947
Prof. Everett Skillings, 1873-1956
Dr. Frederick May Eliot, 1889-1958
Dr. A. A. Roback, 1890-1965

who sought to follow and interpret the path walked by Dr. Schweitzer

CONTENTS

AN UNDERSTANDING OF ALBERT SCHWEITZER

PREFACE

In dealing with *An Understanding of Albert Schweitzer* it has been necessary to quote from many sources inasmuch as the essence of our understanding requires a broad background of facts, events and insights by and concerning Dr. Schweitzer. Specifically, I wish to acknowledge the following sources: the Macmillan Company for permission to quote from the following Schweitzer books: *Philosophy of Civilization; Memoirs of Childhood and Youth; On the Edge of the Primeval Forest;* and *The Quest of the Historical Jesus.* To Harper & Row for permission to quote from John Gunther's *Inside Africa,* Norman Cousins's *Dr. Schweitzer of Lambaréné,* and George Seaver's *Albert Schweitzer: The Man and His Mind.* To Holt, Rinehart & Winston for quotations from *Out of My Life and Thought* and *Peace or Atomic War?* To Beacon Press for passages from Schweitzer's *Goethe; Five Studies; Indian Thought and Its Development;* from Seaver's *Vindication of Schweitzer;* and from Christensen's *At Work With Albert Schweitzer.* To Grove Press for permission to quote from the Schweitzer Foreword to *The Deputy.*

I am indebted to the sources of news items and to columnists and book reviews from the following papers: *Washington Post,* May 1964, for the Russell Howe quotation; *New York Times Book Review,* July 26, 1964, for John Gunther's review, "The Doctor Darkly"; *The Observer,* London, April 19, 1964; *National Observer,* Washington, Sept. 21, 1964, for Carl D. Howard's review; *The New Statesman,* May 22, 1964, for Don Jacobson's review, "Mistrial"; *New York Review of Books,* Aug. 20, 1964, for excerpts of Conor Cruise O'Brien's review; *Ebony Magazine,* December 1964, for quotes from pages 38 and 42; *Washington Star* and Willam F. Buckley, Jr., for his syndicated column, "The Fall of Schweitzer"; Unitarian Universalist *Register-Leader* for Schweitzer's Nobel Peace Prize Address, January 1955, as well as for Dr. Robert Goldwyn's account found in Chapter 9, and for all of Chapter 10 (both appearing in January 1965 issue); *This Week* magazine, Nov. 29, 1959, for "Words to Live By"; and *Iowa Alumni Review* of February 1964. Also selected news items from AP and UPI, as found in *New York Times, Boston Herald, Boston Globe, Christian Science Monitor*. Also to *Time, Life* and *Reader's Digest* for brief passages.

A special indebtedness is owed to Dr. Albert Schweitzer and to his staff at Lambaréné, including Miss Ali Silver, Miss Mathilde Kottmann, Mrs. Lotte Gerhold and Dr. Rolf Müller. Their letters and advice since leaving Lambaréné, as well as helpfulness while there, have been appreciated. Dr. Schweitzer's daughter, Mrs. Rhena Eckert-Schweitzer, has been a help since our first meeting in Lambaréné, and on her two subsequent trips to the United States when we have had opportunities to explore the ideas here expressed. Many "Friends of Albert Schweitzer" have assisted me through their counsels and advice; most notable are Mrs. Julian Rogers, Dr. A. A. Roback, Mr. George T. Keating, Dr. Charles Joy, Dr. Homer Jack, and in England, Rev. Magnus Ratter. I have violated a Schweitzer tradition in quoting letters, but I have done so knowingly. The decision was mine alone. The nature of the public controversy surrounding Dr. Schweitzer seemed to call for a greater exposure of the personal qualities which are sometimes best seen in the subjective disclosures of letters. I have used letters simply to help clarify issues, sentiments and motives, since such have been brought under public scrutiny by others.

I acknowledge my indebtedness to family, friends and associates. In particular to Dr. Dana McLean Greeley with whom I first travelled to Africa and Lambaréné, and who constantly encouraged me. My indebtedness to my office staff and associates, including all with whom I work in the Church of the Larger Fellowship, and most notably to Mr. and Mrs. Rudolf

Amann. Mrs. Amann, who serves as Director of Religious Education, brought a needed perspective at times, and in translation, Rudolf Amann's assistance was most helpful.

The photographic sections are composed of my own pictures taken in Africa, and a section of pictures on Dr. Schweitzer's European background. This latter group of pictures is built around the Hans Steiner picture section from *The Rotarian,* March, 1958, and used with the permission of the editor, Karl K. Krueger, Rotary International, 1600 Ridge Avenue, Evanston, Illinois. To these pictures are added others made available by Mrs. Julian W. Rogers, chairman of the Friends of Albert Schweitzer, 71 Willison Road, Brookline, Massachusetts. The two Erica Anderson photographs are especially appreciated. The Colmar statue by Bartholdi is a French government picture loaned me by Richard Appel of Cambridge, Massachusetts.

A special debt of gratitude is owed the persons who typed this manscript for me: Kathryn Hickey, Darrah Sewell, Helen Todd, and Jeanne Buchanan. Their enthusiasm always added interest and encouragement. However, all responsibility for errors of fact, opinion or judgment is mine alone.

In the final stage of writing, following Dr. Schweitzer's death, the alterations, additions, revisions and re-writing were carried forward with the assistance of Miss Anne Sewell, to whom grateful acknowledgement is expressed.

An author of an independent work is always pleased to find a receptive editor, and I am especially pleased that this volume is being published by the Philosophical Library, so joining the three other worthwhile books on Albert Schweitzer it has published: *The Light Within Us, Pilgrimage to Humanity,* and *Reverence for Life.* Together with these other works, I hope mine helps add to a better understanding of the life and thought of Albert Schweitzer.

G.N.M.

Chapter 1

AN IMMEASURABLE LEGACY

One of the giants of the ages has passed. During the last week in August, 1965, Dr. Albert Schweitzer finished his work. He was pleased with the new buildings, was fatigued by many visitors who streamed to his jungle medical outpost, and had written the pressing letters of grateful appreciation that were on his mind—mostly to those who had helped him over the years. He was saddened by the death of Adlai Stevenson; then came word of the death of Dr. A. A. Roback, *"mein erster Freund in U.S.A."*, and he felt tired beyond belief. Rhena, his beloved and helpful daughter, was at his side. She had matured in the most beautiful and cultured manner a father might wish, understanding better than almost all others his philosophy, point of view, expectations, and plans. Increasingly the Lambaréné Hospital had become her life, and she delighted in telling her father that his granddaughter, Christina, "has caught the Lambaréné bug," and was studying for her medical degree in Switzerland so that she could also come to serve in her grandfather's hospital.

A recent book raised the question of who should be the new hospital director, and its author offered a candidate. Others had suggested the hospital would cease. Consequently Dr. Schweitzer had been asked increasingly, "Who will take over the management of the hospital?" All summer long he had been plagued by this question from many sides. Resolutely, he replied, "The question is not yet pertinent." Yet, he realized, now half way through his ninety-first year, it was time. He called in Rhena and talked with her about the future; after this he felt serenely contented. The new Medical Chief, appointed in February 1965 after serving approximately five years as an experienced member of the Medical Staff, Dr. Walter Munz, was called and he accepted the role of carrying on the hospital, when the time came, with Rhena as administrator.

To the author of these pages, Dr. Schweitzer had confided that his hope was simply to have the physical properties of the hospital in such good condition that "during the first two years when I am no longer in charge, and the necessary transition is made," mundane considerations would not interfere "with the orderly procedures of adapting the hospital to new conditions."

On Monday, August 20, a number of his old friends from Alsace and Switzerland, including the key people in the hospital association who handled his affairs, had arrived. He met them at the landing, and they were instantly concerned over his health. He seemed more stooped, and although in good spirits, they saw he had failed since last summer. Their arrival, indeed, had given him a much needed lift, and renewed his vigor for a few days, but he could not sustain the accelerated pace. Two weeks later there was no question that he was slipping fast, that fatigue had increased. A weariness of body and spirit seemed to join forces in his otherwise serene acceptance of life's inevitable demands. After the Monday evening worship service, he almost entirely ceased any thought of further physical labor. On Thursday and Friday he summoned his driver to visit the different buildings and sections of the hospital grounds. His friends and the staff members observed that he seemed to be looking at every detail of each building, "like it was a last view of his life's work, or—who can tell—as if taking leave," one Swiss friend said. Saturday morning he appeared for breakfast. It was his last attempt to move beyond his room, as though after viewing every nook and cranny of the hospital grounds, this place of gatherings, with his friends and staff, called him for one last farewell visit.

Now, on August 28, 1965, Dr. Schweitzer knew the time had come. He told Rhena that he was tired, very tired, and that she must now prepare for the inevitable end. "When I die," he told her, "notify the family, and the folks in Strasbourg first. You know where the papers are, and will take charge of my will. Think of the patients and the loyal friends here above all others. My funeral plans have been known to you for a long time. It will not differ from any other Lambaréné funeral, and should be simple as well as immediate. I am so glad you are with me."

Now tired, indeed exhausted, he lay down in the simple, aged iron bed and slept. Whenever he awoke he seemed more tired. Gradually, Rhena, Mathilde, Miss Ali, Dr. Munz and the others who looked in realized his strength was ebbing, and the robust, stalwart figure suddenly assumed his full ninety years. It seemed that only yesterday he acted like a sixty year old man; but time had rushed fast in the several days of late August. Briefly, he would rally and think of something he wanted to say. He ate nothing; his appetite seemed gone, although he drank small amounts of cooling liquid a few times. His pulse weakened; his digestive, nervous, pulminary systems, and finally his kidneys, seemed to be slowing their pace and gradually expiring. Then suddenly, on Thursday, during a wakeful period, he thought of a letter he must write. He arose, aided by his faithful companions, sat at the desk, picked up his pen, held it painfully in his hand—tense with the writer's cramps which made correspondence so painful in recent months—and wrote. Exhausted, he nearly collapsed before being returned to bed. He drifted off into a deep unconsciousness which seemed more a coma than a sleep.

The American heart specialist, Dr. David Miller of King City, California, examined him carefully, discussed the situation with Dr. Munz, and Dr. Fergus Pope, and conferred with the senior nurses—Mathilde Kottmann and Ali Silver. His functions were slowly ceasing. The end was clearly indicated. On Friday night Rhena sent cablegrams to his brother, Dr. Paul Schweitzer, 83 (also in poor health, fragile and unable to travel), to his cousins in Alsace and Paris and a few to old friends in Gunsbach, reading: "He is dying, inevitably and soon. He goes quietly, in peace and dignity."

These were the words thought of by others. Almost majestically, it appeared, he had reached the point where death was indicated, and he laid down to die. Later, Rhena said, "Most men would have died sooner, but my father was stronger than most men." In spite of his acceptance of the end, it was clear that the body gave up the struggle slowly and that the mind kept rationally coherent in every wakeful moment. Death finally was described in medical terms. Dr. Miller, the heart specialist, issued to the press the following bulletin: "Death resulted from cerebral vascular inefficiency which manifested itself quite abruptly Saturday, August 28, with loss of consciousness and impairment of cerebral regulation of the cardiac and respiratory functions. For most of the week Dr. Schweitzer remained semi-comatose, gradually falling into a deepening coma. All indicated medical measures were without avail and over the final two days of his life his coma deepened. At no time was there any suffering, and when the end came at 11 p.m., September 4, he passed away quietly in peace and dignity in his bed at the jungle hospital at Lambaréné which he built and loved."

Dr. Miller reported how, while still conscious, his strength ebbing, Dr. Schweitzer lay on the iron bed, shaking hands and talking to all visitors, his deep gray eyes closed and his shock of white hair falling over his brow while he listened to background recorded music of his beloved Johann Sabastian Bach.

One thought of the words of William Cullen Bryant's "Thanatopsis":

> So live that when thy summons comes to join
> The innumerable caravan, that moves
> To that mysterious realm, where each shall take
> His chamber in the silent halls of death,
> Thou go not, like the quarry slave at night,
> Scourged to his dungeon, but, sustained and soothed
> By an unfaltering trust, approach thy grave
> Like one who wraps the drapery of his couch
> About him, and lies down to pleasant dreams.

Others thought of familiar words from Goethe, the cherished poet to whom Schweitzer so often turned. To others the recollection of Schweitzer's own words came back: "Many a time have I, with a feeling of shame, said quietly to myself over a grave the words which my mouth ought to have spoken to the departed, while he was still in the flesh." They thought —if only there were time to tell him what he has meant! In the end he slipped peacefully away. Rhena, Mathilde, Ali, Walter Munz, Fergus Pope and Dr. Miller were present when the slow breathing of a peaceful man was heard no more. Rhena sent by dugout canoe to the Lambaréné Telepostal Communications Center the cablegram to be relayed to the family, and as the sun rose in the misty equatorial sky, word passed in hushed tone from person to person, African to African, westerner to westerner.

The previous evening, as expectation of his impending death spread through the hospital compound, word was carried from person to person by swiftly paddled pirogues, was sounded across the jungle from village drummer to village drummer, and was announced over the Radio Gabon station in Lambaréné. Vast throngs began to gather in the dry parched compound outside of his small room. Whites and blacks together sat on the ground, the steps, the railings, the tree trunks, and waited. Reverently the rhythmic singing of Africans began. At moments of silence, native Evangelists, young men, ancient elders, would arise and speak in moving voices of recollected events that showed the significance or meaning of Dr. Schweitzer's life to them. White nurses and doctors joined in, and told how they had first heard, far across the sea, of the Great Doctor, and been moved to want to come and work with him. "Papa pour nous" became the word of final title used over and over by the African speakers. Gradually, some family groups withdrew to sleep. Others lay down in the clearing, or a nearby shelter. Some stayed all night.

Throughout the morning silent, brooding, tearful crowds gathered in the compound outside his small cell-like room. They stood there silently, queued up in the hope of a last look at the Great White Doctor, as he was known to the Africans, or at Le Grand Docteur, as the white people called him. Together now they joined a common company of consolers one of another. The word passed that he would be buried after lunch in the grove. In the distant background the methodical beat of the drum sent the message to the remote villages still without benefit of telegraph, and along the waterways and river sped motor boats and pirogues carrying the message: "The great white doctor is dead."

A crew of leper workers came forward to dig the grave outside of the window where the still iron cot held the body, and a rough-hewn wooden coffin was prepared not far away. The rough cemetery marker, made of crude cross pieces, was carried out to the fresh mound. Dr. Schweitzer had made it himself. It was simple, unadorned, and like the one that stood over the grave of his beloved wife, Helene. She, with his first nurse, Miss Emma Hausknecht, lay in the little shaded plot outside of the window he so often gazed from as he sat writing at his desk, and here he would be buried. Beyond it was the pen containing the graceful and high spirited antelopes which were the special pets of the famed Doctor. Reverently the body was raised from the bed and placed in the wooden box covered with palm leaves, as was the custom. Eager arms and backs, white and African together, symbolizing, it would seem, the union of the two races in this place, lifted the coffin and bore it to the grave.

Nothing was to be done differently than any other funeral in Lambaréné. The Doctor was unwilling to accept favors in life and insisted on no special prerogatives in death: that was the reason he had fashioned the simple gravemarker himself—he wished no sentimental or ostentatious memorial from some well meaning person or group, and knew the simple marker made by his own hands would forestall the embarrassment of refusal of any subsequent donations. The people gathered at the grave. African mourners began the age old chant in the Galoan dialect: *"Ioanni inina kende kende"* (may you rest in peace). Dr. Munz, walking with Rhena, the sorrowing daughter, and Miss Mathilde and Miss Ali, who were like sisters to Dr. Schweitzer, took their places at the head of the small excavation. In simple words Dr. Munz repeated the service, a few brief words from the old familiar service book, and then clearing his throat, said in French: "God has called him back. The great doctor was like a father. We want to continue his work here in his spirit." The nurses and staff began singing one of the Doctor's familiar hymns from boyhood days, "Ach Bleib Mit Deiner Gnade" (Rest with Your Grace), and the Africans, who speak French rather than German, began to intone a mournful dirge to the accompanying music.

M. Albert Bongo, representing his Excellency M. Leon MBa, President of the Republic of Gabon, stepped forward and with heartfelt emotion paid the Republic's tribute to Dr. Schweitzer: "He was the oldest and most famous Gabonese. The venerable and most venerated citizen of the world has passed away." Bongo went on, "Our soil will accept him as a precious gift. Now, Great Doctor, you will be here forever." A choir of children from the leper village broke into song as the adult coffin bearers lowered the open coffin into the red earth and added additional palm branches as a covering in the final resting of coffin and corpse. Impulsively reaching out to support the arm of Rhena and one of the old nurses was the Ambassador of the United States, David Baine, who had come to Lambaréné from the Embassy in Libreville as the personal representative of President Johnson.

Thus was fulfilled the intention of Dr. Schweitzer, first reported in 1962 by Dr. Dana McLean Greeley, who (in the presence of the author) had invited Dr. Schweitzer to come to the United States to speak before groups in Boston and Chicago. Publicly, Dr. Schweitzer had turned the invitation aside, lightly saying, "You will have to ask me many times, in person and by courier, in letter and by coming, and still I may not answer!" But in the privacy of his room he became serious, and explained, "I am an old man of eighty-seven and do not know what tomorrow holds. Others must go and talk. I cannot. My place is here. I have lived most of my life in Africa and my Africans would not understand if I should leave them at the end and not return. I must show that an Africa good enough to live in is good enough to die in. No, I dare not go abroad again." Thus, it was clear that he never intended again to set foot off the continent, and now that resolve has been fulfilled.

Yet all is not peaceful. The hospital has been reorganized under Dr. Walter Munz as Medical Chief of Staff, with Mrs. Rhena Eckert-Schweitzer as the Hospital Administrator. Changes are certain to come. The author has pointed out in previous writings that there have actually been three Schweitzer Hospitals, rather than one, and would inevitably be a fourth: that which comes into being with the doctor's death. That Fourth Schweitzer Hospital has now begun. First there was the Mission Hospital of 1913; then the post-World War I Schweitzer-Bresslau Hospital which stood independent of the Protestant Mission. Following World War II, a larger, more famous, more international Schweitzer hospital, different from the pre-war hospital, evolved, and today there now emerges the new Dr. Albert Schweitzer Hospital which will be run according to the spirit but without the personal participation of the late doctor.

It inherits many qualities, and also some liabilities. Dr. Schweitzer has been honored in death, as in life; and likewise has been criticized in death as in life. These criticisms the new hospital must come to terms with. Most of this book was written before Dr. Schweitzer died (with his knowledge), although it did not remain for him to see its final completion. He had written, after seeing my review of the area of criticisms, "I found interesting the review of everything that has been written against me that you have also published [i.e., written]. I myself have no overall understanding of these criticisms. I have not replied to any reproach or criticism . . . I have had the great fortune that people have given me the means for founding this hospital and to continue it. I have never bothered with the criticism of my hospital. I did what I considered to be correct, on the basis of my knowledge of Africa."

Those criticisms of which we both wrote have not been silenced by death. Indeed, great newspapers, in their editorial eulogies in the days immediately after his death, took occasion to both praise and criticize him, in spite of the excellent accounts of his life which they gave. For instance, the *New York Times,* speaking editorially on September 6, hailed him and then added: "Less admirable was his treatment of the Africans as children, his autocracy, and his refusal to keep step with medical gains. His hospital was rickety, dirty, and way out of date; yet it was invariably crowded, whereas a sleek and gleaming one nearby had bedspace to spare. The Gabonese preferred Schweitzer because . . . he cared when few white men did. This fact, not his faults, is his true measure."

Similar statements have been made by other papers, recognizing the existence of criticism without challenging or exploring the sources or motivations of such. We propose in the following pages to make such an exploration. Granted, the evidence of criticism shows that Dr. Schweitzer mattered, for if he did not, no one would have bothered or cared. It is doubtful that any notable service can be rendered without some opposition and second-guessing by others. Accordingly, the criticism itself may be a reverse type of recognition of the value of his effort, achievement and contribution.

Many notable tributes were paid to Dr. Schweitzer in death, as in life. President Lyndon B. Johnson of the United States wrote that Dr. Schweitzer's message and example "will continue to strengthen all those who strive to create a world living in peace and brotherhood." He said the doctor "reminded us, by his life and work, of the things that finally matter: that the sick should be made well; that our heritage of religion and culture should be cherished and carried forward; and that all men, of all races, in every part of the world, are brothers. . . ."

Richard Cardinal Cushing wrote: "His work gave the words 'love of neighbor' a new and deeper meaning for our modern world." The Archbishop of Canterbury said: "Few men have had so many talents, and none can have devoted them more unselfishly in the service of God and his fellows. Schweitzer has left a heroic example to his fellow men." In cryptic phrases, Bertrand Russell wrote: "Genuine good and dedicated men are uncommon. Our age is hardly fit to understand them. It certainly does not deserve them. Dr. Schweitzer was both a good and dedicated man."

Thus, his life closed with a paean of praise and appreciation, and a chorus of dissent by those who challenged him. Let us now look at his challenge to us and to our age.

Chapter 2

THE MAN ALBERT SCHWEITZER

Deep in the equatorial jungle of West Africa, where the malaria mosquito is the lord of man, Albert Schweitzer administered his hospital for over fifty years. Everywhere in Africa, except in the West, the white man has been able to survive provided he found the key to harmonious living with the native Africans. In North, South and East Africa the white man had secured his toehold on the continent, challenged only by the African native who wanted to rule and manage his own destiny. In West Africa, between the Congo and the Gold Coast, lay the dense jungle ruled by malaria, and here few white men ventured. Fifty years ago Dr. Albert Schweitzer read of the unspeakable diseases and the suffering of the Africans in a jungle wilderness without a doctor for a thousand square miles. He resolved to return to college, secure a medical degree, and go there as a surgeon to "help repay the white man's debt to the black."

This he did, and for years he was regarded as a successful physician and surgeon, honored and respected by people around the world. It was known that he had a thriving and popular hospital establishment. Later, however, disquieting rumors circulated that all was not well at the Schweitzer Hospital, and that in the African Revolution, where the black African was demanding the abdication of authority by the white man, even the great doctor was under pressures and faced new crises and challenges.

I went to Lambaréné in July and August of 1962. I visited the Schweitzer Hospital and offer this factual report of the conditions, so far as I could see and hear. During my time there I worked with the crews of carpenters and masons, pouring concrete, building forms, and, side by side with both natives and staff members, learning much concerning the hospital management and how both Africans and the staff saw it.

Certainly Albert Schweitzer was a persistent thorn in the side of many people—the myth that would not come to an end. In spite of his half century of service, through which he earned a world-renowned reputation—honored and often held in hallowed respect—he became to some extent a figure of controversy.

Africans were reported to chant: "Jungle doctor, go home!" Military leaders and atomic testing proponents called him a tool of the pacifists, and he himself told me with dismay that some Americans called him a Communist dupe when he opposed nuclear testing, while Communists called him a colonial exploiter in Africa. Orthodox clergymen feared his liberalism as he withstood the swing back to conformity and conservatism during the forties and fifties, when few religious liberals stood by their theological guns. To Roman Catholics he looked like a Protestant saint (or worse, a challenge to the saints), and Protestants feared that he was so broad-minded that he had rejected his evangelical roots. He was a Frenchman who spoke German; he was raised in Alsace and consequently had been reared as a German, but he rejected such German concepts as nationalism, militarism and the state-church principle. In consequence, no matter what camp one was in, one could seemingly find some reason to join the small chorus of protest against a great man who tried, unsuccessfully, to bury himself in the jungle.

Many Africans were reportedly against him; Protestants, fearing his Unitarian "heresy," were against him; nationalists were against him; atomic scientists often were against him; Americans, French, Germans and Russians were often suspicious of his true loyalties. To over-zealous missionaries he was a turncoat, and to the African a foil of the white capitalists. In addition, his hospital had been criticized. Thus some of his friends said that he had outlived his era. Others said: "It is a sad thing to live on after one has become a saint; there is a danger the weaknesses of the man will be revealed."

Achievement – acclaim – oblivion – fame – controversy. So runs the cycle of development in the life of this man whom a national magazine once called "The greatest man in the world." Recently Edward Darling, Managing Editor of the Beacon Press in Boston, was telling how, in the late 1940's, they were featuring a new Schweitzer book when this magazine so designated Schweitzer. Immediately a band was placed around the dust jackets reading: "By the greatest man in the world." When Schweitzer learned of this he was furious. He cabled the Press; "Take it off. Destroy every one. I will not stand for it!" Hastily, Beacon Press sent out the orders to all bookstores to remove the band. "The old man was really furious," Mr. Darling recalls. "He was ready to rip up our contract and refuse to do any more business with us."

This story reminded me of the time Dana McLean Greeley met Dr. Schweitzer in Lambaréné. Dr. Greeley, after some opening exchanges, went on to say, "We salute you as a great theologian, philosopher, musician, humanitarian and citizen of the world."

"No!" Dr. Schweitzer protested furiously, swinging his hands excitedly through the air as though to expunge the words. "All I am is a person trying to live his religion," he cried. He would take no compliment beyond this. He consciously rejected the fame and acclaim that others thrust upon him. One cannot help but wonder: Did he accept the controversy and attacks easier than the praise? I suspect he did, and that he relished the knowledge that no one could confine him into a simple mold, or make predictable his life and his actions.

After I had written him concerning the need to defend his position, Dr. Schweitzer responded, "I never enunciate public explanations in any manner whatsoever. I do not feel obliged to justify myself to the public. This is the simplest way . . . I do not intend to deviate from this independent attitude. It is the simplest and most dignified. I also do not find it necessary to give information about my present views."

With these words, Dr. Schweitzer, who recalled also that he had gone to Africa to make his life his argument, stood on the record of his accomplishments. Simple and great-hearted man that he was, he felt that if he had not proved his worth by the life he lived, mere words would never prove it. In the mills of history this may be so, but in our world of instant opinion, communication is essential for decision making. Consequently, those of us who knew him must speak for him.

There are Dr. Schweitzer's own books, which tend to be subjective disclosures. Such works as *Memoirs of Childhood and Youth, Out of My Life and Thought, On the Edge of the Primeval Forest* and *More From the Primeval Forest* fall into this category.

In a second category of books are those biographies written by those who knew him or who relied almost entirely on his own subjective writing. These books, drawing from his internal view of himself, tend to treat Schweitzer almost as a person in a vacuum so far as social forces and historical events are concerned. He is portrayed as a man of action, and the interaction with the events taking place about him, or his own reactions to social forces, is not clearly seen.

Many of these books present an almost perfect portrayal of the uninvolved man. He ceases being a person of mixed emotions, drives and emotional complexes. He became a plaster saint, not a man of love and fear, with doubts, who struggled to achieve. There is a natural reaction against books in these categories.

Then there came a new category of books about him: those which sought to "debunk." They showed as we have noted, little that was good, and strained to find the weakness and fault beneath the surface. They did in reverse what the abovementioned books did.

The present author is writing a biographical study which seeks to correct these faults from both directions, and to present Dr. Schweitzer as a man molded by his times, interacting, reacting, played upon by social change and experience, and growing through his responses to the trying events through which he lived. This study will seek to go much deeper into the life and interplay that has helped create the Schweitzer we study today in terms of contemporary issues. Much of this material is already written and is now in process of refinement. At the moment there is no adequate modern biography that covers his entire life.

Albert Schweitzer was born in the province of Alsace-Lorraine in the year following the seizure of Alsace by the Germans as a result of the settlement of the Franco-Prussian War. Bismarck was sure that the acceptance of German nationalism in this long established French province would result in economic and national prosperity. However, the French-speaking, Protestant population resisted German absorption, and the inclusion in the German Empire was never fully accepted. Albert, son of a poor liberal Protestant minister, grew up amid the dual loyalties of the divided province. Neither completely French nor German, and, in consequence, with the tormenting sensitivity that tore at his soul, he ended up as a man neither wholly German nor French. Thus he became one of the first clearly defined modern men of universal loyalties, an internationalist who rose above the nationalisms of Germany and France and saw their limitations. From his early experiences here, then, Dr. Schweitzer was inevitably destined to become an international figure rather than a national one, considering his capabilities, accomplishments and articulate leadership.

A word about his family background is in order. On a visit to Dr. Schweitzer once I carried with me a book, *Existentialism and Religious Liberalism,* by a friend, Professor John Hayward. Dr. Schweitzer picked up the book, read the title, chuckled, and asked, "Do you think existentialism is a religious philosophy?" He opened the book and thumbed through it. There was a chapter on Jean-Paul Sartre. He snorted. "Sartre a religious philosopher? You call him religious?" Turning the pages he came to Albert Camus, "Now, here is a religious philosopher, a very profoundly religious man." Then he looked up and said, "I do not mean to be hard on Sartre. On his mother's side he is a Schweitzer. We are cousins, although he has always called me 'Uncle Albert'," Schweitzer disclosed. The relationship of the noted Existentialist and Schweitzer becomes clear in the autobiographical book by Jean-Paul Sartre, *The Words,* published in the United States in 1964 by George Braziller, Inc. As quoted in *Harpers,* September 1964 (Page 49), Sartre explains the relationship. His maternal grandfather was Charles Schweitzer, whose younger brother was Louis Schweitzer, a minister who "carried obedience to the point of likewise begetting a minister, Albert Schweitzer, whose career is public knowledge."

The Schweitzers were, we find as we read this account by Sartre, ministers, schoolteachers, musicians, clerks and various types of intellectuals. With this heritage, the family produced two of the greatest thinkers, epic in stature, of the twentieth century. Hence one can appreciate the accomplishments of the culture which projected both Schweitzer and Sartre on the road to acclaim.

Schweitzer once described three incidents which made a profound impression on him in earliest youth. All are worthy of recall. First, there was his deep concern for animals, which transformed itself into a traumatic experience on one occasion when, in order to be like the other boys, he went along, slingshot in hand, to hunt birds. They lay in wait. The birds settled. The moment to shoot came. Albert took aim, and then jumping up, shooed away the birds. A lad of tender years, he had learned that he could not needlessly kill animal life.

Then there was the Jewish peddler from a neighboring town who drove his cart into Günsbach. To the simple village provincials, the Jewish peddler was a stranger, and the boys would run along beside the cart shouting his name, "Mausche, Mausche." Once Albert joined them (he supposes he did it to show he was now grown up). Noticing the poor man's patient expression, his calm exterior, the freckled face with the embarrassed eyes above the red beard, Albert suddenly felt ashamed, and dropped out of the race beside the cart. Later, whenever he saw the peddler in town, the youth would walk up to him, shake his hand, and walk with him along the street. "From Mausche I learned what it meant to keep silent under persecution, and this was a most valuable lesson," he reported in his *Memoirs of Childhood and Youth.* He also learned not to judge and persecute the Jew, a lesson well learned. Later he was to marry a Jewish girl, Helene Bresslau, daughter of a history professor at the University of Strasbourg. He had become a person without prejudice, able to ignore the bigotry of the area.

A third major impression was made when his family would visit the neighboring seaport of Colmar, where in the public square stood a gigantic statue by a native of that town. Frederic Auguste Bartholdi (creator of the Statue of Liberty) had cast this great statuary to include the figure of the sensitive, sorrowing African slave. The figure strangely moved Schweitzer. He reported that he almost always found an excuse to pass through the square so that he could look at the statue of "The Suffering African," which unfortunately was later melted down for metal in the World War. Its message was to help make clear his summons to service in Africa a few years later.

Schweitzer was also somewhat of a musical prodigy, excelling on the organ under two great teachers—Ernest and Eugene Münch—and later in Paris under Charles-Marie Widor. As such he became a foremost interpreter of Bach. His family's interest in organ building led him to understand ancient as well as modern organs. He was the first to decipher the orchestrations of Bach, meant for medieval organs, thus making possible Bach music on modern instruments. This restored the spirit and lilt to Bach orchestrations so that the music became lively instead of ponderous. The greatest of organ compositions lived again through Schweitzer's musical genius.

Professor Irving Kaplan of the Massachusetts Institute of Technology, and a Fellow of the American Academy of Arts and Sciences, recently told me how he, as a mathematician and musician, began studying the organ books of Schweitzer while serving on the faculty of the University of Chicago. He shared an office with another professor, a physicist, who, he noticed, had on his desk a book by Schweitzer, *The Philosophy of Civilization.* "I notice we're both reading books by men by the name of Schweitzer," the one professor said to the other. "I think they're the same person," the other replied. A third professor came into the room—Professor Tabinhauser, a biochemist specializing in tropical medicines— and said, "That's the same Schweitzer whose reports on tropical diseases I am using in my work here." Thus the rich variety of the contributions of this man stand out. Music, medicine and philosophy—and, of course, theology and ethics—were fields of his accomplishments.

Schweitzer excelled as a student in college, but not without great concentration, for many subjects came hard to him. Torn by family separation and by the theological controversies which found his father in the liberal minority of the ministry, forced to study under teachers who often seemed too pedantic and to sit under preachers who were more orthodox than his father, Albert Schweitzer often turned inward. He lived a lonely, introspective youth in many ways. Yet because of his sensitivity, his brooding, his unique separation due to his family situation, his father's profession, and his own attributes and talents, he was suddenly to find his mind taking wings so that he evolved into a great thinker, grasping eagerly knowledge from many sources, and excelling in many fields. In the University he became an outstanding student, looked upon as gifted and sought out by professors as a man of promise. Great teachers in the University of Strasbourg, then "the most liberal University in Europe," according to Schweitzer, inspired him to further development. He graduated with honors, received the coveted Gall Prize for graduate studies, and earned, as we have said, two additional Doctorates in Philosophy and Theology. He went on to study further at the Sorbonne in Paris, where he earned his Doctor of Philosophy in Music degree, and at the University of Berlin. A decade later he returned to the Sorbonne to complete his studies in Tropical Medicine.

In 1903 he accepted a permanent appointment as Dean of the Theological College at Strasbourg and seemed on his way to a long scholarly life behind the ivy covered walls of this ancient university. It was too quiet a life, however. Excitement came first in lectures, concerts and writing books—the last of which became controversial studies in religion. He was invited to lecture at the University of Cambridge, and found his works being rapidly translated into a score of languages. He studied English with the thought of going to England to lecture at Cambridge on a visiting professorship. Then he decided on a more daring career, in what appeared as a far-off part of the world. Remote Africa called him, and it was said he was going to "bury himself in the jungle." Of course he did not, but that patch of jungle became one of the world's most famous places, a floodlit stage for a great drama.

The man who had excelled in three fields was now leaving them for a fourth. Was he making a saint-like renunciation of the world, turning his back on his accomplishments for an ascetic life of service and sacrifice? Was he running away from battles in three fields where he had not only excelled but had challenged the *status quo,* so that he had become a great dissenter? Had he created a fight he could not finish? Or was he merely a man who needed more than mere excitement, more challenges, new fields to conquer, new outlets for the boundless energy and avid mind that consumed rapidly and eagerly every iota of knowledge spread before it? I suggest it is the latter reason that fired him in this new venture.

There may have been an element of renunciation, there may have been aspects of the dissenter, but never of a coward retreating from the active and controversial European scene. There were elements of the man in need of new outlets, and of the dissenter who had to find a course of honorable service. These reasons we will discuss shortly.

At the height of his success he left Europe, but not without difficulty in doing so. From this moment on we see a life marked by many controversies, but nevertheless a life in which he constantly acquitted himself with honor.

Chapter 3

DOCTOR IN THE BUSH

When Dr. Schweitzer came to Africa in the Spring of 1913 he seemed far removed from the world of the white man's culture. The river boat made its slow way, huffing, puffing and rolling up the Ogowe, stopping every now and then at a village to take on a fresh supply of cord wood for the steam boiler which provided locomotion. The Doctor and Helene looked attentively at the Africans and their native villages. Schweitzer was also impressed with the white men, so much like the fabled Trader Horn who once lived up this river at Lambaréné. There seemed to be a slow deterioration—almost a degeneracy—taking place of whites, Africans, and their villages. Some of the lumber men and traders who were passengers explained to the Doctor that alcohol, with which black labor was paid, brought about the break-up of the old village disciplines. Others told him it was the effect of trade, which took Africans out of the tribal pattern. Still others blamed it on religion, which undermined the basis of tribal beliefs and substituted a white man's God that did not have jungle roots. Dr. Schweitzer took all these ideas to heart and thought about them, and in time was to come to believe all were parts of the picture. Truly, the time to repay the white man's debt to the black was overdue.

He began now to understand that his role would not be to set up a white man's version of a hospital, but to create a hospital that would serve best the needs of the African, so that he would not play a conscious part in destroying African tribal culture. Over the years many a trader, lumberman and colonial officer was to leave the Schweitzer hospital, shaking his head and thinking, "This doctor is a 'nut.' He respects the Africans, believing their culture is equal to ours. Imagine not wanting to upset the superstitious beliefs of African natives." Yet Dr. Schweitzer's respect for the culture of the African, arising out of his studies in comparative religion and anthropology, marked him as a unique white man. In spite of the changing public opinion on Africa, Dr. Schweitzer's attitude is still unique. He has changed little in both his appreciation of the African culture and his expectations of it. He never joined any movement, whether of whites or blacks, to usher in an era of rapid transition which would cut the roots of the African. He respected the tribes and the religions on which their folkways rested. One who "goes it alone" never wholly supports, nor is he supported by, either side in a controversy. This was to be Dr. Schweitzer's destiny.

At the Lambaréné mission station he was disappointed to find that the arrangements promised had not been made, the facilities not provided. The missionary in charge of arrangements was not even there, having returned to Europe. Consequently, Schweitzer set up his first hospital in a fowl house, which he had to clean by hand so that the refuse and clutter of its ousted inhabitants did not remain. Here, with a recruited African youth, Joseph, as an orderly, and Mrs. Schweitzer as nurse, he performed his first operations, and became the great "Oganga" (fetishman) to the Africans, the Doctor whose knife took life and restored it. He was the first doctor in a thousand mile area, and natives, Europeans and missionaries turned to him for help.

Ministering to his patients had its difficulties at first. Once, he found his trusted orderly, Joseph, turning away some of the patients. Joseph was an unusual youth. Schweitzer had been promised an orderly, a school teacher by the name of N'Zeng, trained in French as well as in the native tongues. However, he was not at the mission when the Doctor arrived, so Joseph was selected as he seemed to be a bright, alert youth with a natural aptitude for hospital work. Having served as a domestic for some European families, he already knew French.

He often created problems for the Doctor, however. Once, for instance, he whispered, "This patient you should not see, Doctor."

"Why should I not see him, Joseph?" the Doctor demanded.

"He has a worm in his cutlet and the fetishmen and medicine men have refused him. He is going to die and nothing can save him. His family are numerous and powerful and they will bring reprisals if the fetish or medicine is unsuccessful," Joseph explained.

"Joseph, that is why I have come. There are people who suffer and they may die, but, in the meantime, I might make it easier for them. They may die with less pain, if they are to die, because of my medicine. And then, the white man may know how to cure what the fetishman does not. I will see him," he said, looking at the emaciated figure on the litter gasping convulsively for breath.

This was one of the Doctor's great tests and one of the trials he continually had to go through. First of all, he needed to be resolute against his friends who, knowing the ways of the jungle people, tried to turn away the fatal cases. No witch doctor would take them. He should be as smart as they were. Then, he needed to build his own reputation in those early months so that the natives would have confidence in his medicine and his skill. Fortunately, all of his early operations were successful.

Nothing amazed the African more, in those now remote days of 1913-1915, than to learn how the White Doctor would "kill" a person, cut him open, take something out, sew him up and then bring him back to life—with no more pain! This was a truly marvelous wonder that even the best of the fetishmen could not do. Indeed, the Doctor had superior powers and great magic.

Dr. Schweitzer was often puzzled by certain developing patterns which he had not expected. Helene would prepare appetizing meals for the patients; but on his rounds hours later, the Doctor would be dismayed to discover that none of the patients had eaten. First he thought they were too sick. Then he decided that Helene's ways of cooking made the food strange to the African, and so he engaged African cooks. Still, not even the convalescing patients would eat.

"Joseph, why will the patients not eat? I know they are hungry," the Doctor once said to Joseph.

"Oh, that is part of the ways of our people." Joseph began to explain. He then conveyed to Dr. Schweitzer the native belief that most sicknesses were caused by poisons mixed in with the food so that they were taken into the body. "So our people will eat nothing not prepared by their own families or a trusted friend," Joseph concluded.

"But there is no poison in our food!" the Doctor exclaimed.

"Oh no, it need not be that kind of poison. In fact, the most dangerous poisons are evil thoughts and evil wishes. If the person cooking or mixing food merely thinks such thoughts, they are stirred into the food and then taken into the body. Most sickness is caused by these evil thoughts entering the body with food, our witch doctors and fetishmen say," Joseph explained.

"Very well. We will have each cook his own food. Tell all the people to bring a member of their family to cook for them henceforth. We shall issue the food. We shall cook nothing for them." Thus the Doctor, with his characteristic decisiveness, developed one of the distinctive patterns that were to separate this hospital from all others. Even today, one can see at Lambaréné the little fireplaces where the many families prepare their own food.

After this, Dr. Schweitzer took other steps in developing the adaptable African hospital he has made famous—not a European hospital, not a city hospital, not a regulation hospital, but a workable jungle hospital. The family feeding program and other details were gradually added. As he was adding them and moving more and more into his hospital work, he was cautiously observing and developing his own philosophy of the relationship between black and white, African and missionary, primitive and civilized. He saw in Lambaréné the meeting of cultures; in his person and his service, the meeting occurred. How best should the cultural transition take place?

Many whites, including those at the mission, felt that there were peculiarities in the African's outlook and his way of life —his abandon, his living for and in the moment, his trustfulness that everything will work out, his belief in spirits, charms and magic—that interested and often amused them. They did not see these as parts of a genuine culture deserving of respect. Rather, they thought the white man had culture and the African was without culture. However, to Dr. Schweitzer it was already clear that the African had a culture that was self-respecting and should command respect as well. Unlike the missionaries, the colonial administrators and the industrial developers, Dr. Schweitzer did not believe it was the white man's duty to superimpose a different culture on the African in the name of civilization.

This single factor was to make Dr. Schweitzer a minority of one, a white person standing apart from almost all other whites, often misunderstood by other white men; and perhaps by Africans who expected a single, uniform reaction from all white persons and were puzzled that Dr. Schweitzer did not respond that way.

The unhappiness and distress felt on his arrival that the hospital had not been prepared, turned out to be good fortune for Dr. Schweitzer. Those first weeks in the chicken coop had shown him that a hospital building should not be conventional if it were to serve the Africans who were coming to him in such large numbers. He would design his own hospital. He began to sketch out his ideas and made check lists to go by. As a result, from the first, the Mission Hospital was different. The mission plans called for a hospital to be built on the top of a hill, but Dr. Schweitzer realized the folly of this plan. The patients came by boat and many could not walk. To have to oversee the carrying of patients up the hill in the glare of the sun would be difficult. Often a canoe put in to shore and simply deposited the sick person on the bank. In this instance, the total responsibility became the Doctor's. Too, the supplies, which came every two weeks now by steamer, were in large bulky wooden cases. How much simpler if they did not need to be carried up a hill. Finally, he discovered that the top of the hill did not have any more breeze than was at the bottom.

In fact, the hot sultry air of this Equatorial climate was like an oven, top or bottom. The sun, moreover, beating on the roofs of buildings in the open made them like great incubators. There would be no protection from the sun on top of the hill. Furthermore, he and Helene would have the long climb in the sun each morning and afternoon.

How much more simple to have the new hospital at the foot of the hill in the grove near the landing. Here, it was a short distance to carry patients. Here, there was a coolness from the water. Here, there was shade from the trees. Dr. Schweitzer mentioned this to Mr. Christol and Mr. Ellenberger, two missionary teachers. They saw his point instantly, but shrugged their shoulders. Such management details were worked out and voted on by the Missionary Council, or Synod, and there had been much discussion over the location of the hospital.

"When does the Council meet again?" the Doctor asked.

"It is the meeting we are going to in two days," Mr. Ellenberger answered. "You are welcome to come along and present your proposal. In fact, you might get some action on moving ahead with it." It was agreed that Dr. Schweitzer would attend the conference to be held at Samkita.

Dr. Schweitzer met with the missionaries and won agreement for his plan as how best to build his hospital. From then on, they allowed him the necessary freedom to set up his hospital as he saw fit—even though it was still on missionary land—particularly since he made clear he planned to pay his own way and would sign notes to refund any advances made or credit extended to the hospital.

The two main tribes served by the hospital were the Galoas and the Pahouins. The Galoas were one of the old, long established tribes of the area, a people whose way of life had changed little from prehistory until after the coming of Schweitzer. This was their ancestral tract. They were a more docile people than many; this, in fact, was almost their undoing. When the French came, the Galoas had the area to themselves, but an inexplicable migration of the Pahouins, or Fangs, from the interior began to take place. Fighting their way into the area, the Fangs, who were a cannibalistic people, waged fierce warfare on the meeker Galoas. These cannibals were of a strong personality, intelligent, more advanced in warfare, and quick at adjusting and making the adaptations required for instant survival as they invaded. Their greater skills, as well as their belligerency, were leading to the extermination of the Galoas when the French took matters into their hands and stopped the warfare and invasion, decreeing that both tribes should share the land. An uneasy peace developed. The members of the two tribes would work together, but they never actually accepted one another.

Once, Dr. Schweitzer asked some natives to carry a litter for him. Looking down on the patient, they replied, "He is not of our tribe," and they refused to give assistance. They had a very real sense of brotherhood for those of their own tribes, and they would obediently assist a fellow tribesman whether they knew him or not, but brotherhood did not extend over tribal lines. Another example of this division was that a Galoa would refuse a blood transfusion until he knew for certain that it was from another Galoa.

Joseph was a Galoa. N'Zeng, who finally arrived, was a Pahouin. Dr. Schweitzer found it very helpful to have an interpreter for each tongue as well as one able to exercise tribal authority over their members, making the work of the hospital run more smoothly.

Dr. Schweitzer continued to cooperate and attend the Missionary Conference. Once he attended a meeting where a missionary was lecturing a group of newly-converted Christians. The missionary was holding forth on the need of the Christian to give up the African ways, which included having more than one wife. The missionary was laboring the point of "sacrificing the joys of polygamy." After he had several times referred to the joys of polygamy, Dr. Schweitzer gently tapped him on the shoulder and, with a chuckle, whispered, "My brother, what makes you so sure that to have more than one wife would be a joy?"

Not only were the missionaries responsible for the transition of tribal authority taking place, the lumber and other trading firms were also hastening change. For instance, the lumbering companies found it easier to recruit laborers from interior tribes. They brought them out "on contract" in units and returned them to their native territory after the stipulated period, usually two years. This policy was carefully supervised by the Colonial administration; nevertheless, a marked deterioration in the traditions of the men usually took place. Away from home, families, tribal customs and beliefs, living in billets and barracks compounds, they tended to take to steady drinking. They would become undisciplined and would often wander off to the villages of the nearby tribes. Here they were not subject to tribal laws, and since they were unlawful they became a menace. With the beginning of the World War the lumber companies hastily disbanded services, and the Colonial government did not have time to supervise the labor migration policies, as attention was turned to military and related matters. In consequence, numerous laborers of distant tribes were turned loose and became migrants. Chief among these tribes from the interior were the Benjabis, but in a short time there were several other tribes also pushing into the towns and village lands of the older Fangs and Galoas. Such tribal members created disciplinary problems at the hospital as well.

In addition, the Christian conversion of the indigenes was also apparently hastening the disintegration of the tribal pattern, as the superstitious taboos on which the elders relied were now looked upon by Christians as falsehoods. Accordingly, the older pattern was disintegrating under the impact of twin forces: Christian proselytizing within the villages and the external breakdown of the trade and labor economy of the colonial order. There was much concern on the part of Africans as to how to cope with these changes.

The elders and medicine men dealt with the situation in a hideous way. A secret organization was formed—controlled by them—which was called the Leopard Men. Its purpose was to put a stop to the breakdown of the old tribal ways. Before the young men of the tribes could be influenced by the missionaries they were secretly initiated into this order, which demanded blind and unquestioning allegiance to the fetishmen and elders. Given a secret initiation at night, then dressed in the skin of a leopard and with steel claws that cut into the flesh they were sent forth to attack the non-believing Africans. A fearsome reign of terror set in. Dr. Schweitzer was called upon several times to treat patients who had been critically injured and mangled by the metal claws. The standard technique of attack was for the Leopard Men to try to sever the carotid artery, as leopards do; when they succeeded, there was nothing the Doctor could do.

The young men inducted had no choice; they did not volunteer. At a tribal gathering they were unsuspectingly given a potion to drink. Afterwards they were told that it was the leopard potion and that they were now members of the Leopard Men. They feared the Leopard band and dared not resist. They had to submit to the destiny that was chosen for them. Their loyalty was first tested by an order to bring a sister or a brother to a grove as a sacrifice. The next time, they had to do the killing.[1]

Once, Dr. Schweitzer recalls, the government decided to stamp out the Leopard band and arrested ninety men on suspicion. They administered poison to one another and all died in prison rather than divulge information.

As stated above, an opposite parallel to the disintegration Schweitzer saw was the recruitment of other promising young Africans to serve as native missionaries; they thus lost the opportunity to become effective community and tribal leaders when confirmed or baptized. At one meeting of these missionaries, Dr. Schweitzer was called upon for a comment, in spite of his pledge to be mute. Accordingly, he joined with them in the discussion, expressing his view on a matter of religion. He was promptly rebuked by an African convert who responded by saying that the conference members should not take the Doctor's opinion into account "since he is not a theologian, as we are."[2]

Dr. Schweitzer's concern for the natives as a physician was

1 Schweitzer, *On the Edge of the Primeval Forest,* pp. 124-125.

2 Schweitzer, *Out of My Life and Thought,* p. 169.

his only real concern. Here it was that he most truly related to his Africans. The number of people with heart disease astonished him, and they were equally astonished that he could diagnose their disease. He recalled with delight the visit of an old woman when he first arrived to establish the hospital. Stethoscope in hand, he listened to her heartbeat, examined her chest and back, asked a few questions, and then prescribed digitalis. When Dr. Schweitzer turned away, she looked up at Joseph and said, "Now I know we have a real doctor. He knows that often I can hardly breathe at night, and that I often have swollen feet, yet I had never told him a word about it, and he had not looked at my feet."[3]

Among the patients there are some who demanded payment for their recovery. One, N'Gonde, had a severe case of sleeping sickness, running a high fever, and becoming so disturbed mentally that he had to be restrained. On being cured, and returning to normal, he charged the Doctor: "Now that you have cured me; buy me a wife."

The work at the hospital became more demanding with the passing years. More and more patients came and more and more building seemed required. He and Helene were often worn out with exhaustion, and he suffered several minor attacks of sunstroke. Huge ulcers began to grow on his feet, so that it became painful for him to walk or wear shoes. He realized he must be careful or he would lose his feet. He began to talk of the need to return home so as to replenish the health of both, for Helene was having fevers at increasingly shorter intervals. Then the river steamer put into Lambaréné one day with the terrible news: the Austrian Archduke had been shot and war was declared! War in Europe! For a moment it seemed a long way off, but shortly thereafter the Commandant sent black soldiers to place Dr. and Mrs. Schweitzer under house arrest. They, as German nationals, were under suspicion.

This was the starkest irony. Here was Dr. Schweitzer, a son of loyal French Alsatian parents, educated in Strasbourg, Paris and Berlin. He came from a tiny province of forced dual

[3] Schweitzer, *On the Edge of the Primeval Forest,* p. 31.

allegiance. He, who had no strong sense of nationalism, was suspected by the French of being a loyal German, and so was interned as a prisoner of war. The paradox was that he had put Europe, with its nationalism, boundaries, borders, and suspicious ways, far behind him. Now, thousands of miles from that upsetting Franco-German borderland, he found himself on another Franco-German border—that of Gabon-Cameroon, or to be more clearly expressive, that of the northern border of French Equatorial Africa which lay along the southern border of German Cameroon. Here, almost immediately, the French and German colonial troops were locked in battle. As the fierce fighting between French and German soldiers drew to a stalemate, the commanders began recruiting African soldiers to fight on their respective sides.

Dr. Schweitzer, a man of bi-nationalism, now found himself caught in the same bi-national border struggle he knew at home. Was there no escape from nationalism? Only internationalism offered hope, and his active mind was led inexorably to the conclusion that all nationalism is wrong.

Dr. Schweitzer and Helene were kept under house arrest for several months, the hospital closed. However, constant supplications to the District Commandant had to be made on behalf of critically ill persons, and special permissions for the Doctor to see and administer to such people were constantly granted by the vexed and harassed French official. In consequence, he held an inquiry into the loyalties and activities of Dr. Schweitzer. The result was that the Doctor and his nurse-wife were adjudged to be "non-political" and were allowed limited freedom, so long as the Doctor restricted his activities to medical services in the district and confined his movements to the hospital, Protestant and Catholic mission stations, and the nearby villages he was previously accustomed to visit on professional calls.

Ogowe natives were now being recruited for military service by the French army and Dr. Schweitzer, in consulting with the patients, learned just how confused they were by this distant war which was upsetting their lives in Africa so much.

"Why, Doctor," he was asked, "do the white men who

brought us the gospel of love not practice it among themselves?"

Again he heard mutterings about the fact that only a few months before a native was executed for shooting a white man. Now the black men were being trained with rifles to shoot white men. How could this be? It had been a crime for an African to possess a gun or ammunition, except for special hunting permits; but now Africans were being trained as soldiers in order to kill one another. This reversal of moral code seemed especially difficult to understand, and the African who had to learn this from the white man was therefore confused.

One old African observed that there was a difference between the white man and the black. The whites were more cruel, because they simply killed and left the dead, whereas the Africans, in their tribes, would kill other men only when they were hungry—for in those early days some of the African tribes still practiced cannibalism.

One old chieftain who came to the hospital asked the Doctor: "So many already killed, and still they do not meet for a palaver. Already twelve men for our area alone are killed. How can the other tribe ever pay for so many killed?" He was referring to the local custom that after a skirmish, the tribes would meet in a palaver—a huge talk-feast—and come to terms, setting a price for each person killed, which had to be paid for by the victors (thus the losers often seemed to win!) . Dr. Schweitzer could not help but feel that this way of warfare—called more primitive—might actually be more civilized.

These events had a deep and depressing effect on Dr. Schweitzer. He saw the European, and in time, world war, from the objective point of view of the African. There was something wrong with it. In the so-called civilized world people were not free to make personal judgments, nor to question and doubt the wisdom of the war policy. In Africa, Dr. Schweitzer was influenced by the African, who saw the war as a great folly and waste. Its effect, and the influence of these "natives," on Dr. Schweitzer was fundamental, and never wore off. To his last days he was influenced by the recollection of the greater humanity and civilization of the African native. That the African had a gentleness and kindness, and a better sense of balance (the true meaning of justice, tempered with a fellow-feeling, which might be called love or mercy), influenced Dr. Schweitzer's attitude right up to his death. It conditioned his thinking on Africa, for it was his hope that the African movement toward civilization would not involve the loss of the human values of Africans, even while developing the harsher, impersonal attitudes of the industrialized Western world.

It was at this time, too, that Dr. Schweitzer observed the happenings in Africa from the perspective of the meeting of two cultures. Paradoxically, this stood out most at the time when intermingling was breaking down. In the absence of developed channels, Dr. Schweitzer saw the inroads made by the intermingling of the white and African cultures.

Most of the white men in Africa had returned home. For the most part, only administrators and military officers remained. Schweitzer, therefore, was one of the few whites uninvolved with the course of the war who stayed on. He spent three years in district confinement before being removed to a European prisoner of war camp, and saw that the irresponsible withdrawal of European leadership left the African floundering in a sea of uncertainty. It suddenly became clear that African self-reliance and self-confidence was only in relation to the new culture of the Afro-European commingling. Without the dual poles, the African was immobilized.

As a result, Schweitzer became convinced that the African and European civilizations had become so interlocked that no simple solution such as withdrawal could work. Whether one liked it or not, the transition and development of the African culture as a part of the world culture had gone too far to turn back. The old world of the African primitive had vanished, and a new world of cooperation between black and white was evolving until the exigencies of the war brought it to a halt.

In the modern period following the Second World War, neither the European colonialist nor the new African liberator could understand the position of Dr. Schweitzer, who held a complex view of two cooperating cultures rather than of an either/or culture. In 1914, as a result of these observations, Schweitzer ceased to believe in a colonial solution as adequate for Africa. But for him this did not mean an independent and uninvolved African solution. Something was necessary to bring the two together. It could not be the missionaries; not the military; not the traders; not the economic exploiters; not the white settlers; not the African tribal elders; and not the new sophisticated African who ignored the deeper roots of African culture. Africa was changing, and a new cultural orientation must result. He did not know what it was, but it would not be found by falling back on the easy, old answers.

The old Africa, he knew, held part of the answer: the tribes, the elders, the folkways, the old village and territorial rights and ways. They could not just be swept under the table and a full culture—one of substance—for the new Africa developed. Likewise, the long period of colonial liaison had made contributions which had to be maintained. One could not ignore the transitional era and honestly expect to evolve a new system. Consequently, those who move rapidly, who rely on the future without the past, who depend on emotional rather than rational responses, felt Dr. Schweitzer's wider view to be old-fashioned. On the other hand, the old-fashioned colonialist and missionary felt he had been too progressive and moderating in his views to have been on their side. Thus Dr. Schweitzer suffered the fate of the individualist and the liberal: he was condemned by both sides and found all camps arrayed against him because he was not unequivocally in any. This is the price of integrity for the comprehensive thinker.

Dr. Schweitzer, who was broken in health, and his wife, who was suffering from tropical fever, were finally, and mercifully, interned and returned to Europe in 1917. His health did not improve until the early 1920's, as he languished in one prison after another. Mrs. Schweitzer's health never did recover, and she spent the rest of her life infirm although she lived until the age of seventy-five.

Schweitzer during this period faced one other great crisis:

his mother had been walking along a country road in Alsace when a galloping troop of German cavalry rounded the corner and trampled her to death. This brutal, accidental death bore heavily on the Doctor, along with all the other sorrows and sufferings brought by the war. So many of these events were unspeakable, yet he found it difficult to share his deep sense of loss and frustration with others.

War was monstrous. Although the slow period of his recuperation, which took five years, seems long to others looking back on his life, he needed the full time to recapture his sense of values, his interest, and his spirit, so that he could then move back into the active life he knew and loved. Not the least important aspect of this recovery was the birth of his first and only child, a healthy and happy daughter, Rhena. She would mean much to his wife, too, the Doctor knew, and he was overjoyed.

After the birth of Rhena, Dr. Schweitzer returned alone to Africa. Helene could not face the trip at this time, but she was so filled with apprehension that she might stand in the way of Albert doing what he had to do that she insisted he go.

Schweitzer's decision to return to Africa came when he was forty-seven years old, and many friends urged him that he was now too old for such an active life. He had reached the point at which others must go and serve, while older men enjoyed the honors of old age, he was told. That was forty years ago! Schweitzer, as usual, heeded his own counsel and returned to Africa, filled with hopes of not one hospital, but several. Instead of curtailing, he hoped to expand his activities.

Unfortunately, his old hospital had been reclaimed by the jungle. Revitalizing it took all his energy and effort for several years. First, he rebuilt it on the site at the Mission, but he had hardly completed the task when he realized this was a mistake. There was not enough land; the mission was not large enough for its own needs, let alone his. In addition, his concept of an independent hospital, and of his right and need to be independent as a person, led him to apply to the District Commandant for a concession of his own further up the river. This was granted, and he began the slow, arduous task of building out of the virgin jungle his own hospital on his own land. One entry in his journal was significant: "All the money advanced by the mission, I had paid back." He moved off, unbeholden to any group, and established his independent hospital without obligations.

Now began the work in the second Schweitzer Hospital, and from 1925 until World War II he carried on a modest, slowly developing institution in an Africa that was, outwardly, slowly developing along the colonial pattern, while inwardly it was seething with unrest. Superficially it appeared that the Schweitzer Hospital was not making rapid progress, but actually the Doctor was developing and extending the patterns, altering and improving according to the pragmatic principle by which he worked (rather than by the manuals of operation of medical societies).

Since 1924 Dr. Schweitzer had been recruiting a staff of doctors and nurses from around the world. At first they came entirely from Europe. His first assistant was a university student from England, Noel Gillespie, but afterwards medical doctors and registered nurses began to join the staff. One of the advantages of having a larger staff was that research into tropical medicine was now possible, much to the stimulation of the doctors in residence. Also, the great foundations, such as the Rockefeller Foundation, began to send them experimental drugs and equipment for testing. As a result, the hospital moved into an area of usefulness in the service of all mankind through medical research.

Great specialists began to visit the hospital, giving of their skill in the heart of the jungle and in turn learning from the specialization of the resident doctors on the medical frontier of jungle life.

Still, one could never forget that this was a jungle hospital. The new hospital became something unique among hospitals. Here was an African village composed of many tribal units, a commissary, plantations, a landing, barns, pens, groves, roads and a well. It was to grow into a throbbing, pulsating African community where one could find on any day at least seven hundred African patients, with many more family members awaiting them. In a recent count there were over seventy-five buildings (now on cement foundations). It takes eight tons of food—bananas, manioc and rice mostly—to feed the Africans who come to the Schweitzer Hospital.

Operations keep the staff busy up to the last moment on Mondays, Wednesdays and Fridays. The operations fall into three main categories: ulcers and hernias, gynecological, and general surgery. Then there are emergency operations at any hour of the day or night. The putt-putt of the electric generator alerts the entire hospital community, for it is used only to supply power to the trim and neat operating theatre.

Many Americans and Europeans are surprised when they visit the hospital. There are no "Quiet Zone" signs; no "Hush, Please" posters. This is not the quiet, tiptoe-type of hospital where employees are in uniform and move quietly through silent halls, but a bustling village of Africans, farm animals and monkeys. Dr. Schweitzer has created for the African a unique and amazing hospital—a village where he can feel completely at home. There is no other place like it in Africa, no other like it in all the world.

Here as blacks and whites mingle, there are many languages heard: Galoa, Fang and other tribal tongues; German, French and English. Seldom are you out of hearing of a confusion of tongues in this international settlement.

The doctors and nurses also represent this widespread background. In recent years there have been six doctors on the staff, coming from three continents: Europe, Asia and America. The dozen or more registered nurses come mainly from Europe, with some from the United States, and at the time of Dr. Schweitzer's death were under the supervision of Mademoiselle Mathilde Kottmann and Mademoiselle Ali Silver, who had been with Dr. Schweitzer since the hospital was finished. There are also practical nurses who are locally trained Africans on the staff. There are usually twenty to two dozen on duty in the hospital. These nurses are all males and usually are married men. They have plantation sites allotted to them which their wives run. Those who have more than one wife have large plantations so that they can raise more fruits and vegetables, with which they augment the salary paid by the hospital.

In 1962, Joseph, then retired, lived in a small cabin. He would walk up to a visitor and say, "I am Joseph. I speak English. I was Dr. Schweitzer's first medical assistant. I am the same age as *le Grand Docteur*. Would you like to have your picture taken with me?" Joseph was then a little, wizened-looking man with a kind and gentle face, and an unassuming air. One wondered if he was really as old as Dr. Schweitzer—nearly ninety. It was a pleasure to shake his hand. Thus does the continuity of the hospital go on.

There are other continuities. There is an old cemetery on the grounds, lying between the main hospital buildings and the new Leper Village which was built with the Nobel Peace Prize money. The graveyard is a decadent looking site beneath high palm trees. It was our habit to pass it by until one day when Dr. Schweitzer's daughter, Rhena, asked if we had looked at the stones. "Most of them are Moslem stones with a crescent on them and Arabic inscriptions. My father thinks that a century ago a Moslem trading party passed here, was caught in the smallpox epidemic, and was buried here."

"However, there is another stone there," added Miss Silver, "that you will want to note. It is that of the aged cook of Count de Brazza, the explorer. Many years ago Dr. Schweitzer met him on the wharf at Port Gentile. He was old, nearly blind, lame and destitute. Dr. Schweitzer took pity on him and brought him here, where he lived out his life. He is buried in the cemetery here." Thus in this hospital are the tangible evidences of the passing phases of life in Equatorial Africa.

Other stones stir one's recollections of the history of the hospital. They stand in a small grove outside of Dr. Schweitzer's window: one for Helene Bresslau Schweitzer, who died in 1957, and one for Mlle. Emma Hausknecht who, after a lifetime of service as second nurse to Dr. Schweitzer, died and was buried on the hospital grounds. Now a third stone has been added—that of the Doctor, on the spot he selected.

Chapter 4

SCHWEITZER MISUNDERSTOOD

On June 4, 1965, a letter from Dr. Schweitzer to *Life* magazine was printed which concluded with the paragraph: "Do not be concerned with the stupid articles which have been published about me and my hospital. The most important thing for me still is that my hospital is doing well. And I am very happy to be able at my age to go on working here." One who corresponded with Schweitzer would wish that he could have seen the actual letter—whether in French or German—to determine the implications of the word translated as "stupid," for our English word "stupid" infers a degree of culpability not usually implied by *Le Grand Docteur.* Rather, one might assume he meant merely "the incomprehensible articles," for he had written in that vein several times to this writer. He had "no grasp of the point of such articles" he wrote in February, and again in April he wrote me, "I have no overview of what my critics are trying to say." Those of us who were privileged to know him found a friendly and sincere, almost self-conscious, man who tended to efface himself rather than imperiously disregard his challengers. The unfortunate result of the publication of the friendly letter, evoked by his gratitude to *Life* for its cover story about his ninetieth birthday (see the issue of February 19, 1965), is to suggest his dogmatic rejection of criticism. This is far from the case.

When another editor recently spoke of Schweitzer as an "autocratic Prussian," he was resorting to the stereotype of the German mentality held by many Americans and applying it to Schweitzer. As will be noted, Schweitzer was an easy-going Alsatian (to apply another stereotype), one of those bi-nationals who have for centuries been torn between French and German loyalties. He grew up with a bi-national cultural synthesis that is at home in either country—or in all countries. Alsatian intellectuals have long been among Europe's leading internationalists.

An understanding of Schweitzer begins with the knowledge that much written about Dr. Schweitzer is inadequate. To understand this great man, we must begin with a fresh, new approach. In fact, much of the criticism, rather than being "stupid" or willfully erroneous, is merely the result of the failure to find in the Doctor the type of person one was led to expect. With death, perspectives begin to clarify.

Before discussing what one may expect, let us first look at the critiques, so that we can bear these in mind in the pages which follow. Undeniably there was a popular flare of misunderstanding arising out of the criticism concerning Dr. Schweitzer and his hospital in the spring of 1964. For many people it began on April 19, 1964 when *The Observer,* London's controversial and sensational newspaper, ran a five column spread that proclaimed: "Attack on the Legend of Schweitzer." In this article John Ardagh reported his interview with the author of a critical attack on Schweitzer, announcing in an opening sentence: "The legend surrounding the great Dr. Albert Schweitzer is about to be struck a furious blow." He then summarized an interview with a Mr. McKnight, without doubting either his conclusions or observations. *The Observer* told us that "Mr. Gerald McKnight presents a detailed and highly critical analysis of his [Schweitzer's] life and his fifty years' work in the jungles of Africa." The book in question was *Verdict on Schweitzer,* published in London and New York in 1964. Who is Mr. McKnight? He was identified as "a Fleet Street journalist." The sagacious and critical Conor Cruise O'Brien, Chancellor of the University of Ghana (who reviewed the book in *The New York Review of Books* of August 20, 1964) noted that "Mr. McKnight's writing has the worst features of the kind of British journalism which formed it; cockiness, ignorance, carelessness, prurience, innuendo, and lip-service to the highest moral standards . . . he pursues the Man with a dull, pertinacious hostility, an obsessive anxiety to find discreditable interpretations of the most innocuous biographical data, which can only make one reflect how much greatness must still smoulder, even on the wreck of Schweitzer, to arouse so much envious malice."

An even greater popular authority is the noted world news reporter, John Gunther. In *The New York Times* of July 26, 1964, Mr. Gunther wrote:

"Gerald McKnight, a youthful British journalist, has now written what sets out to be a complete job of telling the 'truth' about Schweitzer and rendering a 'verdict' debunking him from top to toe. The author deserves credit for trying to put the record straight and wanting to give us a soberly considered estimate of Schweitzer. Unfortunately he does not succeed. Schweitzer is certainly a legitimate subject for a seriously critical book but this is not it.

"Mr. McKnight has a peculiar hit-and-run attitude toward his quarry. He is dealing with a colossus among men, a true giant however idiosyncratic and testy, but he does not come to real grips with him. He darts forward, then draws back, as if abashed by his own temerity in tackling such an elevated subject....

"I do not think Mr. McKnight gives enough attention to the concrete achievement that is to Schweitzer's credit—the single-handed creation of a bush hospital from scratch, no matter what the failings of the hospital may be. Schweitzer may be tyrannical, arbitrary and a fuss-pot, but his accomplishment has elements of the titanic. No one can take away several aspects of his greatness as a 'universal' man. Nor does the author seem to have much conception of the realities of contemporary Africa."

The authoritative book reviewers warned us that Gerald McKnight is not competent in his craft or knowledge to accomplish the purpose intended, and they discovered that he fails in other ways. Gunther writes, "Moreover, Mr. McKnight is not quite candid with the reader. He never tells us how much time he spent in Lambaréné or how many hours (or minutes) of talk he had with Schweitzer himself."

Mr. Carl D. Howard reviewed the book for *The National Observer,* Washington, on September 21, 1964. He noted that "Although he claims to have visited the Lambaréné hospital, for example, Mr. McKnight unashamedly mentions a certain building there, 'which has a notable plaque, so I am told.' But if he's indifferent as an observer, Mr. McKnight is worse as a researcher. Why hint that the charities aiding Schweitzer have great wealth, including many unused or misused funds? Why not get facts and figures from the nonprofit organizations he mentions?

"And finally, there is Mr. McKnight's awkward prose to contend with. For example, he ponders on the possibility of a successor at Lambaréné hospital . . . '*if* [my italics] Schweitzer were to die.' "

At the time, one of the most highly respected reporters on the African scene was Don Jacobson, who reviewed the book for *The New Statesman.* His review of *Verdict* was entitled "Mistrial," of which a portion follows:

"Dr. Schweitzer is regarded by many in Africa and elsewhere as a controversial figure, whose attitudes to the Africans he works among are riddled with the simplest colonial-style prejudices, whose medical practices at Lambaréné are outdated and cranky, and whose views on nuclear disarmament are not necessarily of any greater importance than those of, say, Mr. John Osborne. Stories have circulated about the eccentrics and misfits who have been donated to the hospital from all parts of the world. Now, out of what he implies to be a disinterested devotion to the truth, Mr. Gerald McKnight has come along to ask 'the plain question: is Schweitzer a saint or a fraud.

"The question is, of course, not 'plain' at all—as the author insists throughout that Dr. Schweitzer is not a saint, the reader is then left to come to the conclusion that the partriarch of Lambaréné must be a fraud. Not that Mr. McKnight ever actually calls him a fraud: he specialises, rather, in smears and innuendos, and in putting slanders into the mouths of (unnamed) others, and then backing away from them with a show of judicious impartiality. His qualifications for writing on Dr. Schweitzer are obscure: he appears to know little about Africa (he remarks with an air of faint surprise on the fact that the Gabonese 'are obviously at home in European clothes') and still less about medicine, music, theology, philosophy or missionary work.

"Mr. McKnight is too much of an unintentional clown to be a really effective character assassin. But he does his laborious best. Dr. Schweitzer admits to the impression made upon him by Wagner's music—'the music,' Mr. McKnight ominously reminds us, 'that late inspired the Kaiser's and Adolf Hitler's goose-stepping soldiers.' He devotes several pages to the adventures of a woman with the Jamesian name of Mrs. Clent, who left her home in Weymouth for London in order 'to meet and study Jewish people,' living meanwhile on a diet of oranges and honey; she then set out on a bicycle to Lambaréné, which she reached after many mishaps and accidents. 'Her strongly-boned face shone with a release of reverence at the mention of the Doctor's name. Furthermore, her skinniness and wounds had vanished.'

"Perhaps the most disagreeable thing about the book is that, though he is ready to use accusations of colour-prejudice against Dr. Schweitzer when it suits him to do so, and to suggest that the rise of independent African states has made work like the Doctor's superfluous, nowhere in the book does the author ever mention actually speaking to any of the patients in the hospital or to the African medical assistants, or asking the views of Gabonese government and health officials concerning Lambaréné. Instead, he makes free with terms like 'natives,' 'savages' and 'primitives.' It never occurs to him that the final, complicated verdict on Dr. Schweitzer's work in Africa will have to be made by a black man, not a white man."

The attitude of most informed readers tended to support Mr. Howard of *The National Observer* when he wrote that "Like a pint-size dog that yips but never snaps, Gerald McKnight's *Verdict on Schweitzer* barks a lot but never sinks its teeth into anything solid," and of Geoffrey Godsell of *The*

Christian Science Monitor whose review was entitled "Failed Debunker." McKnight's effort to belittle, puncture or debunk failed in its intention.

Nevertheless, there is something here to be looked at by those who wish to make an honest appraisal of Dr. Schweitzer. Every coin has two sides, even as does McKnight's writing. Dr. Schweitzer's life also did, although it is not necessarily seen or comprehended by Mr. McKnight. Essentially, McKnight has said that the back side is counterfeit; the more objective observers have denied that thesis. Yet there are areas of concern which McKnight tried, but failed, to adequately expose. Writing objectively, but without malice, we shall try to expose and comprehend the issues surrounding this complex man who perhaps cannot be simply reduced to "either saint or fraud." McKnight's study may assist us because he has seized upon areas of concern—some petty, some laughable, some mistaken; some flagrantly erroneous, and some too complex for easy solution without a thorough background in the cultural and ideological factors involved. Because in some of these areas I have already a predisposition to certain conclusions, I will again quote from some of the reviewers. My own critique appears in the subsequent chapters.

We have already seen the insufficiency of Mr. McKnight as a critical authority. Nevertheless he has opened up a discussion of Dr. Schweitzer as medical man and hospital administrator, and as a human being, whether "saint or fraud"; of his religious ideas; and of the relation of Dr. Schweitzer to the emerging independent African culture. How do the reviewers assess his judgment? First let us look at the human Schweitzer as seen by McKnight.

Gunther noted that "The general tone is that of a man with a tremendous lot of revelation to make who cannot quite bring himself to the point of doing it. This leaves the reader with the feeling that he has not much to give. There are also minor examples of naivete. . . . Mr. McKnight describes Dr. Schweitzer's career and daily routine, writes—without much point—about the women in his life and seeks to add him up as musician, philosopher and theologian. He mentions his autocratic attitudes, depicts the atmosphere of oppression prevalent at Lambaréné, and brings up a number of details that indicate the hospital hasn't changed much in the last 10 years. He calls the sanitary conditions 'atrocious' . . . He touches repeatedly on the point that Schweitzer, whether saint or 'fraud,' probably created his hospital not merely for the public good but to save his own soul by a long-continuing public penance."

Conor Cruise O'Brien dealt with the human factors of Schweitzer as they emerge in McKnight's study, and found amusing the account of McKnight's privation in the process: "Schweitzer receives him, the old man permits himself the unsanctified luxury of sitting in a 'chair padded with several layers of foam rubber,' while leaving the young journalist to sit on 'a hard wooden stool.' His diet also is pretty lax: he has two hen's eggs 'specially reserved' for him each day: 'Thus the jungle doctor whom the world sees as a saint ensures that his strength is kept up whatever happens to anyone else.'

"The old man's depravity is in part explained by the tendencies of his early youth. He liked Wagner, a fact which when interpreted by Mr. McKnight gives us this sinister picture: 'The music that later inspired the Kaiser's and Adolf Hitler's goose-stepping soldiers made a thunderous impact on the young man sitting alone in the stalls.' Schweitzer's responsibility for the war was, however, even closer than this. The year 1905, in which Schweitzer gave up his academic post to study medicine was, as Mr. McKnight tellingly establishes, 'nine years before Europe was brought to war by his Kaiser.' Having noted this chronological link with Hohenzollern aggression, we are not surprised to find that Schweitzer prefers 'savages and cannibals' to his own family. Did he not refer, in an autobiographical work, to the 'pain of parting,' from Africa, although he had not used these words about leaving his wife and daughter in Europe?

"Proof enough for McKnight on Schweitzer certainly. Schweitzer's early life was a sad business altogether. Snobbery and sex reared their ugly heads. He is entertained by Countess Melanie de Pourtales: 'How cosy and titillating these aristocratic associations sound . . . and how hard it is to imagine them culminating in a life of abnegation in the jungle!' He goes for walks with a Mrs. Herrenschmidt. Mr. McKnight licks his lips: 'Together we can imagine them roaming the student quarter and enjoying the piquant life of the city. Though he makes no excuse (sic) or explanation for alluding to her in an exclusive paragraph of his memoirs except to say that they 'saw a good deal of each other,' doubtless Schweitzer's usual reticence about everything private in his life is reflected here.'

"One could forgive the debauchery, the writer seems to feel, if the fellow wasn't so furtive about it. Even after he went to Africa his goings-on have something to do with sex, although Mr. McKnight cannot, greatly to his disappointment, find out just what, except that the nurses are women and tend to admire Schweitzer. Some of them are a little odd, and all have come a long way. One lady's journey, by bicycle from Abidjan to Gabon, gives Mr. McKnight an opportunity to display his Africamanship:

" 'When the ship reached her port of destination, Mrs. Clent trundled her bicycle down the gangplank, mounted it, and rode towards the jungle. Her path to Schweitzer lay across nearly 1,000 miles of jungle, bush, scrub, wild-land, bad-land, swamp, river, tundra, forest, lake, and plain. The tribes she would pass among contained many with savage reputations. Cannibalism is not extinct, by any means. (While I was in Lambaréné, there were seven convictions for it in Sierra Leone, farther up the coast.) A few miles east of Abidjan Mrs. Clent crossed the border into Ghana. Farther in the same direction she entered Togo; then Dahomey, Nigeria and the Cameroons. Here she turned south, though by now she had parted with her map and went only in the directions given her by friendly natives. Having cycled her way across the high Cameroon and skirted tiny Spanish Guinea, she entered Gabon. The end of her journey was unbelievably in sight.'

"On this journey the lady was hardly in more danger of being eaten by cannibals than of freezing to death in all that 'tundra.' Apart from mosquitoes and saddle-sores, the greatest risk she ran was that of being knocked down by a truck on the busy stretch of highway between Sekondi and Accra.

"*Verdict on Schweitzer* has its comic aspects but the total effect of the constant drip of feeble spite is most depressing. Take, for example, the chapter boldly entitled 'The Tragedy of Madame Schweitzer.' Here the writer wrestles flabbily with meager data to get such holds on reality as these: 'Schweitzer (in his autobiographical writings) deliberately avoided mentioning Helene whenever possible. This could have been, and is, believed by his admirers to have been, praiseworthy reticence . . . Nevertheless the rigorous skirting of Mme. Schweitzer's role in events he was describing gives an altogether different impression from chivalry. And where she is mentioned the reader can be pardoned for wondering what special reason lay in the Doctor's mind for choosing to reveal her.' If one starts from the assumption that Schweitzer is a thoroughly bad hat then it is clear that, whether he leaves her out or puts her in, he must have some discreditable motive, which, if one had sufficient imagination, one might even find. What the tragedy was I have been unable to discover from Mr. McKnight's account except that Mme. Schweitzer like other mortals was sometimes ill, may sometimes have been lonely, probably found the tropics hot, and eventually died. The culminating passage is a quotation from Norman Cousins' *Dr. Schweitzer of Lambarene* 'January 1957. The first time I saw Mme. Schweitzer I could see she was not well. The blue veins stood out in her forehead and seemed stark against the pure whiteness of her skin . . . When she spoke it was with considerable effort. Her breathing was labored . . . Once I saw Mme. Schweitzer start out across the compound, her weight bent forward on her stick and her whole being struggling for breath. I rushed to her side and took her arm. She looked up at me, somewhat puzzled, as though I did not know the rules of the game at Lambaréné.'

"What a brute Schweitzer must have been—the whole context of this chapter in McKnight's book implies—to reduce his wife to such a condition! The message loses some of its impact when one realizes, by comparing dates, that this description is of Mme. Schweitzer a few months before her death, which took place in Zurich at the age of seventy-five."

Don Jacobson, also used to the rigors of African austerity, found amusing the passages that dealt with the "discomforts" forced on the younger McKnight before the older doctor. Jacobson gives us this summary paragraph:

"He suggests that Dr. Schweitzer 'fled' to Africa because he was afraid of the repercussions aroused by his theological works; that his views on the building of organs and playing of Bach are disputed by many authorities in these fields (this also appears to Mr. McKnight as evidence of some kind of moral failure) ; that he is autocratic and arbitrary in all his administrative decisions; that he wasn't sufficiently thoughtful about the health of Mrs. Schweitzer or the upbringing of Miss Schweitzer; that he assiduously courts the limelight; that he enjoys the adulation of his wealthy female admirers; that his reflections on civilization and progress are deplorably pessimistic; that he hasn't performed any surgical operations for many years; that he eats an egg every day, though others at Lambaréné go without them for weeks on end; and that when he gave Mr. McKnight an interview he sat on spongerubber cushions while Mr. McKnight sat on a hard wooden stool—'the hardest stool,' he repeats with feeling a few pages later, 'I have ever had to sit on.' "

Thus are we presented the caricature of Schweitzer, a parody on the personality and nature of one of the colossi of the age, one whom the noted biographer Stefan Zweig called "too complex" to write about after spending a day with him.

In reporting on the petty and fantastic characterization of McKnight, we have opened doors to other issues: the question of the standards and nature of the hospital. Is the hospital "as bad" as the critics say?.

One of the more critical accounts was not written by the English writer, McKnight, but by an American newspaper man, Russell Howe, who wrote in *The Washington Post* in May 1964 about "The Press's Myth of Dr. Schweitzer." By this time the McKnight book was on the stands in London, and various other columnists were joining the fray against the previously unblemished Dr. Schweitzer. Mr. Howe wrote: "As, month by month, fresh evidence of the appalling conditions prevailing at the Lambaréné settlement is dragged before the public gaze, there may be—there is already—a tendency to forget that the Schweitzer myth was not created by Albert Schweitzer. . . .

"Schweitzer himself has not written of his hospital, except for scattered mentions in some books with titles like *On the Edge of the Primeval Forest;* he has never claimed to be doing anything saintly or exceptional; he has never once denied the criticisms that have appeared, over the past decade, of his 'village.' The most that can be laid against him was his failure to disclaim the deceptive halo others cast about his photogenic silver locks.

"Ten years ago, I took a dugout canoe across an equatorial river and visited the hallowed horror known to the world as Schweitzer's hospital. What I saw then is now common knowledge to any reader of any paper: the filth and squalor, the domestic animals defecating in the 'wards'. . . .

"Today's visitors are still shocked, although some of the characteristics of the hospital have been reformed. The staff is no longer required to be all Teutonic: French doctors are now accepted, and, wonder of wonders, African nurses. Some 'wards' now have cement floors on which patients can eat and keep their clothes.

"In 1954, writing factually about all this was almost taboo in the press. Describing Lambaréné meant saying that Schweitzer was an eccentric in a field—medicine—in which eccentricity can be tragic . . .

"In a travel book written that year, the chapter on Schweitzer's 'village' had to be emasculated so many times, to preserve some of the sanctity of the myth, that the desire to take the entire chapter and ram it, page by page, down the publisher's throat, was almost irresistible."

One wonders if Mr. Howe would be surprised—or care—that when he wrote this account there were only two Germans on the staff of two dozen European, American and Asiatics serving the hospital—with another two dozen Africans of semi-professional rank for all "outsiders" serving there.

At about the same time *The Boston Herald's* George Frazier (making no pretense of having read the book by McKnight, but quoting John Ardagh's account in *The Observer,* London) reported to his readers that the Schweitzer hospital "was the most unkempt place of its kind" in Africa. He went on to say: "What Mr. McKnight . . . achieves, however, is a grave indictment of Albert Schweitzer as a human being. 'Face to face,' he says, 'Schweitzer emerges as an autocratic political persuader rather than a humble doctor'."

Obviously, Dr. Schweitzer and his hospital were under powerful attack from many sources—"as an autocratic political persuader" running an "unkempt place." Now William F. Buckley, Jr.,—a columnist appearing in numerous papers across the land, author, editor, controversialist, conservative and anti-liberal—joined the list of debunkers attacking Dr. Schweitzer. Buckley reported, in a column entitled "The Fall of Schweitzer," that Gunther and McKnight had disclosed the "appalling conditions" existing in the hospital. His greatest criticism was against Schweitzer as man and Christian, which we will discuss later.

What did John Gunther have to say about the hygienic conditions at the Schweitzer hospital? Here was an outstanding reporter. For the past decade his *Inside Africa* chapter on Schweitzer, "A Visit to Dr. Albert Schweitzer," has been regarded as the most critical statement in print by Schweitzer devotees. *Reader's Digest* had condensed it by deleting unfavorable observations. Presenting only the best side of what Mr. Gunther reported was an offense to many impartial people. In fact, *Reader's Digest* did in reverse what friends of Dr. Schweitzer believe McKnight did: deleting what mars the true picture to maintain a pre-conceived stereotype. An illustration from *Inside Africa* will show what we mean. On page 726 Gunther reported: "We peered into the operating room one morning; it was startling to be able to look right in from the courtyard. On the table lay a naked Negro, his abdomen streaming with blood. I looked more closely. It was not blood, but mercurochrome. The doctor who performed the operation —it was a routine hernia—came in to lunch an hour later. He had not had time to wash up completely and, in his shirt sleeves, sat down with his arms still scarlet with mercurochrome up to the elbow." I heard this passage quoted once as though Gunther had reported that the doctor's arms were dripping with mercurochrome instead of stained with it. This passage is also used by those who wish to give an unfavorable impression of the hospital's medical facilities. However, the next sentences, which end the paragraph, are then omitted. Gunther immediately went on to write: "I do not mean to indicate by this that surgery at Schweitzer's hospital is rough or incompetent. It is not. Standards are high." Of course, it is this last sentiment that *Reader's Digest* highlights, omitting the gory details above. Was it not better to see Dr. Schweitzer's effort from the balanced point of view of both sides, as given by Gunther?

With the publication of McKnight's book in the United States, the *New York Times* asked John Gunther to review it, which he did. His review, "The Doctor Darkly," included a reminiscence of Schweitzer and the hospital. He wrote:

"This reviewer spent a week as a guest of Dr. Albert Schweitzer at his celebrated jungle hospital in Lambaréné in 1953. I was doing road work for my *Inside Africa.* I have never forgotten that experience in the bosom of the tropical jungle. It had moments of utter enchantment and revelation. I admired fully the magnificent record of the Great Doctor's quadruple career (music, philosophy, theology, medicine), and I have been impressed ever since by the quality of his unique and indeed formidable personality.

"I did not quite succumb to every blandishment of the Schweitzer myth, which in that day was accepted without reservation almost everywhere. I do not think that what I wrote about the great man 10 years ago was offensive, and, although I pointed out some of the oddities in his bristly character, my tone was sympathetic rather than overly critical.

Dr. Albert Schweitzer, in a photo taken in his garden in Günsbach, Alsace.

The town of Günsbach, Alsace. Dr. Schweitzer's house is the one in the extreme right foreground.

Entering the town of Günsbach. The Schweitzer residence is a little way down this road.

"The Suffering African" statue of Bartholdi in the central square of Colmar during Schweitzer's youth. This statue strongly influenced the young boy's sense of African injustice, was later melted for arms in the World War.

One of the famous buildings in Colmar, the Pfisterhaus.

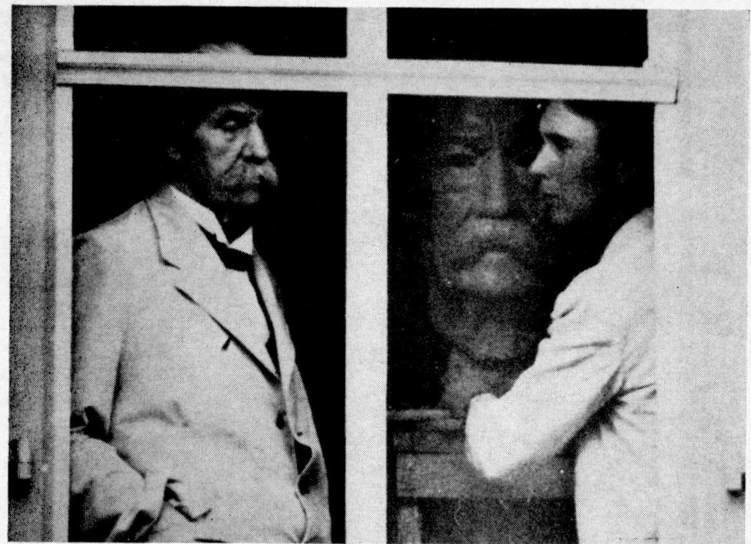

Georges de Boulogne adds finishing touches to bust of Dr. Schweitzer, Günsbach.

Dr. Schweitzer at his writing table.

Two famous sons of Alsace who became renowned internationalists as well as musicians—Charles Munch, Conductor Emeritus of the Boston Symphony Orchestra, and Albert Schweitzer, after a concert in Strasbourg, June, 1954.

Madame Rhena Eckert-Schweitzer talks with her famous father at a reception. She has now succeeded her father as Hospital Administrator in Lambaréné.

Dr. Schweitzer's music room, with the harmonium he played. The painting shows him in his early years as an organist.

I did, however, dare to say that the Schweitzer hospital did not quite live up to its reputation as the model of a Christian community, and that the doctor seemed to have no intimation of what was going on in the rest of Africa and had scarcely ever in his life talked with an adult African on adult terms.

"Of course the doctor is an extremely touchy subject. I discovered this at once when my book came out. Schweitzer partisans, inflamed with fury, flew to his defense, and I was roundly chastised by the old man himself—mainly because, if my memory is correct, I wrote that he looked like Buffalo Bill, which indeed he does. Schweitzer addicts could not believe that some of the things I said were true—for instance that the physical accoutrements at Lambaréné left much to be desired and the doctor's medical techniques were somewhat backward. The 'Schweitzerines' could not endure to have the image tarnished.

"In those days, comparatively few observers had much knowledge of the nationalism then beginning to burst out. It shocked readers when I said that Schweitzer, although he had devoted most of his life to Africa, had little but contempt for the nationalist movement and indeed took the line that white colonial rule, benevolent if possible, should presumably go on forever. I was not arguing whether African nationalism was good or bad, and certainly the Master of Lambaréné had a well-earned right to his opinion."

Conor Cruise O'Brien, a resident of West Africa, cooperative and familiar with the attitudes of the newly independent rulers of that vast continent, highlights many of the areas of criticism regarding the hospital. He wrote:

"It is more than fifty years since Albert Schweitzer went to Lambaréné, in what is now Gabon, to practice medicine and found a hospital. In that time he has become a symbol, to a large white public, of altruism, self-sacrifice, and dedication to the Negro. . . . The Africans in whom he is interested are the 'simple' ones—the more primitive the better—and for their sakes he keeps his hospital also 'simple,' that is to say primitive. The photographs, which are the best part of *Verdict on*

Schweitzer, show this clearly.

"There are several—though far from enough—modern hospitals in Africa, and it seems clear that Schweitzer's fame has brought him enough financial support to turn Lambaréné into such a hospital. He keeps it as it is because he believes that 'simple people' would not come to a modern hospital: an opinion disproved by the experience of the modern hospitals in Africa. When he first came to Lambaréné in 1913, Schweitzer and his wife were running real risks, enduring real hardships, and making a real contribution to the health and welfare of those among whom they chose to live. Today, by refusing to admit that anything has changed, this proud and obstinate old man has become a tragic anachronism."

Mr. O'Brien endures the fate of all white men who would stay and work in the New Africa: he must constantly be on the alert to dissociate himself from colonialism, paternalism and the missionary movement if he wishes to hold status with the new African elite. Unfortunately, all white men who have survived the era of colonialism are constantly under suspicion. Mr. O'Brien, therefore, is courageous to even write about Dr. Schweitzer's hospital and his attitudes toward Africans.

He presents well, nonetheless, the conditions and assumptions on which modern African decision will rest: Africa has "gone modern," there no longer are "simple Africans," but all Africans must be considered sophisticated citizens of a new order descending from and revolutionizing the older Africa inherited from colonialism and the missions. Schweitzer had not moved forward rapidly enough in affirming the new Africa and in disclaiming any connection with the old order under which he functioned for half a century. Furthermore, he called the world's attention not to a modern medical facility in a great metropolitan area or university center, but to a humble backwoods "bush hospital" serving the rural rather than the assimilated African who has accommodated himself to modern living conditions. Good public relations would call for a world lens on a modernized institutional situation rather than on this "simple" village clinic.

All aspects of these issues are discussed in separate chapters which follow. The other areas of criticism, beyond those of the hospital conditions and of the modern attitudes on African independence and the vanishing remnants of colonialism, will likewise be fully discussed by us. Before turning to the fuller accounts, however, we need to have some rebuttal to the controversial nature of the charges which we have already advanced, as found in the discussion taking place in the spring and summer of 1964.

After *The Observer* article by John Ardagh appeared on April 19th, that paper's audience was pleased to find comments from readers the following two weeks, one by the most critical mind of our day—Bertrand Russell—who wrote as follows:

> Sir, I wish to endorse all that Mrs. Urquhart says in her letter about Dr. Schweitzer. It is not a very great discovery that Dr. Schweitzer's single-handed effort to help people blighted by disease may be superseded by modern medical facilities. It is obvious, however, that technical progress always carries with it the price of impersonal machinery, which is devoid of the humanity that a dedicated individual provides through his own action and example.
>
> I have never been averse to examining people and issues with a view to seeing how things are, rather than how they are reverently said to be. It is unpleasant, however, to find noble things studied without the desire to understand, and with the object of flourishing a lack of understanding before those who would never undertake them.

In America, Mrs. Miriam Rogers, Chairman of the Friends of Albert Schweitzer, wrote to *The Boston Herald* expressing her disappointment with Mr. Frazier's account:

> I was surprised that he would take the word of one author, namely Gerald McKnight, and his *Verdict on Schweitzer* verbatim.
>
> With his broad perspective of people, books and world affairs, he must know that any great world figure is often

criticized and, truthfully, is often inconsistent and paradoxical.

There is nothing new in Mr. McKnight's book against Dr. Schweitzer. Many have visited Dr. Schweitzer, and in spite of the untidiness of the hospital (which is actually a native village with hospital facilities where patients can live in their own craals with their families and possessions), have come away loving and admiring him.

I myself have visited Dr. Schweitzer, as have many local people.

Mr. Frazier spoke of the myth of Albert Schweitzer and of saintliness. Dr. Schweitzer is certainly no myth, and his books reveal how real, practical and knowledgeable he truly is. He is no saint, he is very human indeed. When *Life* called him 'The Greatest Man in the World' he disliked it intensely.

His attitudes toward the Africans must be respected, whatever they are, after 50 years of serving them. They love and respect him, including workers, some of whom have been there 25 or 30 years, ailing patients and children.

I only wish Mr. Frazier could be in the presence of Dr. Schweitzer for even a short time, to gather his own opinion.

That the efforts of a single man and that a jungle village for "those who bear the mark of pain," as Schweitzer described it in one of his autobiographical accounts, will be superseded by institutional or governmental progress is obvious and is not discreditable. The nature of the hospital—its patterns and services—we will explore fully in later chapters. Suffice it here to note that critics to the contrary, Dr. Schweitzer's work had been appreciated and recognized by his own country's leadership. The hospital is located in the Republic of Gabon, and the highest honor of that Government, the *Etoile du Gabon*, was presented to Dr. Schweitzer by President Leon MBa, the great African statesman and intellectual who heads the Gabonese government. M. MBa was present also at the 90th Birthday festivities in Lambaréné for Dr. Schweitzer on January 14, 1965. His attitude expressed in the Appendix is also significant.

Others, too, support the concept of the simple family and tribal style hospital—a form of healing which takes sick and anxious people at their own cultural level without trying to remake them into urbane persons while curing them. For instance, *Ebony* Magazine, December 1964, carried a feature account of the Nigerian psychiatrist, Dr. Adeoya Lambo, an unusually gifted and creative leader of his people who, coming from a small African village, studied at the University of Birmingham in England and returned to Nigeria to practice. The article and pictures stress that he concurs with Dr. Schweitzer's view on simple surroundings for successful therapy. It says (page 38): "One of the unique features of Dr. Lambo's psychiatric clinic villages is the fact that all patients live with normal members of their families who are on hand to cook and attend to household chores. Dr. Lambo believes that his patients' contact with their normal relatives and neighbors contributes significantly to their recovery." The caption under one picture (page 42) reads: "At preliminary examination, psychiatrist asks woman patient probing questions. His theory, that Africans respond best to treatment in familiar surroundings, supports Dr. Schweitzer's much criticized views." To McKnight, O'Brien, Gunther and others, this simple, family-style hospital development of Dr. Schweitzer led to criticism of the hospital. It gave the hospital an "unprofessional" and disorderly appearance due to the family-style life carried on beyond professional restraints.

William F. Buckley, Jr., a spokesman for the reactionary elements in Western society, took a different point of view in making his major attack on Dr. Schweitzer. He wrote a column, appearing in dozens of papers in the summer of 1964, which I quote in part because of its monumental ignorance of the sequence of events in Dr. Schweitzer's life, and in part because of the basis for his criticism of Schweitzer—a criticism which must be taken into account because it may be the most serious one of all. Mr. Buckley wrote:

> Dr. Schweitzer, after all, is quite a man. It might even be

said that he is the 20th Century's Promethean man. First he was a musician, specializing in the performance on the organ of the works of Bach and the author of a definitive two volume work on Bach. Then he entered a medical school and became a doctor. Then he announced himself (sic) a theologian, earned a degree, and wrote copiously on theology.*

But of course the most conspicuous thing he ever did was suddenly to remove himself from Europe, which lay prostrate at his feet, to a tiny inaccessible corner of Africa, and there in Gabon, he set up a hospital where for several decades he has ministered to the sick and leprous.

What a climax to an already great career! The engines of approval wheezed into play and before long the doctor's name had become sacred. He won all the routine prizes, including the Nobel Prize; biographers lined up to write his life and colleges begged him to come around for honorary degrees.

And then the reputation began to falter. John Gunther reported several years ago and in his book, *Inside Africa,* that the hygienic conditions in Dr. Schweitzer's hospital were appalling. The reaction was two-fold: 1) that there was no reason to suppose that John Gunther would recognize a hygienic condition if it hit him over the head; and 2) if there was a little grime or soot in the hospital at Lambaréné, so what?, so isn't that like criticizing the molecular structure of the clay used by Michelangelo in shaping the Pieta?

But then, Dr. Schweitzer said some extraordinary things during the Katanga crisis of two years ago, which will be

* Do we, in passing, need take time to point out that Mr. Buckley is confused about the sequence of Dr. Schweitzer's life? He was the Dean of the Theological College at Strasbourg University from 1903, and did not make his decision to become a doctor of medicine until 1905, after his major theological work, *The Quest of the Historical Jesus,* was already completed. Accordingly, one is surprised to find Mr. Buckley reporting: "Then he entered medical school and became a doctor. Then he announced himself a theologian, earned a degree, and wrote copiously on theology." By the time he became a doctor, his major theological work was already done, and his "great renunciation," as some biographers called Schweitzer's decision to change careers, was the renunciation of already established careers in the academic, theological and musical worlds.

recalled as that master stroke of U.S. diplomacy wherein we decided that the Congo was not big enough for Moise Tshombe. The doctor—who heretofore had been utterly available to the Establishment for congenial political remarks, who had done yeoman work for the pacifist and anti-nuclear groups, who had even defended the regime in East Germany, said he thought it quite foolish for the West to take dogmatic anti-colonial positions in Africa, that anybody who had eyes in his head could see that the Africans were not prepared to govern themselves.

I gave the doctor about a year or two, which is about how long it takes for the machines to stop, after the brake is applied. Now a British journalist, Gerald McKnight, has written *Verdict on Schweitzer,* which is a venture in demolition, and leaves Dr. Schweitzer's reputation canted over at about the same angle as the Tower of Pisa. It is the breathless conclusion of McKnight that probably in his entire life Dr. Schweitzer has not conducted an adult conversation with a single African.

During all these years there was a small redoubt of people who held out against the transfiguration of Dr. Schweitzer, but their complaints against him were different from those that actually succeeded in felling the myth. They were trying to say that Dr. Schweitzer was no theologian, that his fabled formula for successful (if not happy) living lay in a 'reverence for life' of which he considered himself perhaps the world's outstanding exemplar, greater than Jesus, Who was a good enough Jew, but Who made some dreadful mistakes, which Schweitzer would apparently not have made. As an individual practitioner of many of the preachments of Christianity, however, he was most certainly a saint, having given himself over so completely to the practical service of others.

A not uninteresting study could be made, contrasting the liberal-conservative attitudes towards Dr. Schweitzer, and identifying the poor old gentleman's Achilles' heel: which turned out to be not his dangerous self-struck theology, but his irreverence towards the holy causes of anti-colonialism and permissive egalitarianism.

The essence of Mr. Buckley's rambling attack is grounded

in the discovery that Schweitzer wasn't a tool of the Establishment, that his medical practices did not follow the standards of Mr. Buckley, and most of all, that he held a "dangerous self-struck theology," whatever that means. Quite obviously, however, the theological variance of Dr. Schweitzer is most disconcerting to Mr. Buckley (author of *God and Man at Yale*), who found offensive Schweitzer's concept of Jesus "as a good enough Jew" who made some mistakes.

Undoubtedly, as we shall discover, many of those who accept the criticism of Schweitzer do so because in the realm of ideas he is not a clearcut representative of the established religious views of the major faiths, anymore than he is of the military establishment.

In discussing the basis for the attacks on Dr. Schweitzer, Buckley's final point stands out: Dr. Schweitzer's major shortcoming was that his ideas were at variance with those of the Establishment. Over and over Mr. McKnight, too, seemed to be murmuring this in a secretive whisper which said, "But, are you aware that this man is a non-conformist, who accepts all the honors of the Western world and rejects its religious, ideological, mass communication, and popular ideas?" It was the scandal of Schweitzer—to McKnight, Buckley and others—that in going to Africa he rejected European civilization; that in leaving the ministry of the State Church for the profession of medicine he rejected the narrow rut in which the Christian Church was caught; that in becoming non-political he rejected the superficiality of the political institutions of our time; and then, in becoming an ardent spokesman for the banning of nuclear bombs and their testing, he defied the political order and status quo of the western world. All arguments break down to one: Schweitzer was not an organization man; he fitted no mold, conformed to no prototype, and did what he 'jolly well' pleased without counting the consequences. Like Confucius at seventy, what pleased him "did not transgress the right."

Now let us turn to a detailed study of this great non-conformist and individualist who walked his own path and see to what extent he fits our expectations of a great man, a free man, a person of integrity who in challenging our society gave us a plumbline by which to test its direction.

As we have said, these criticisms may themselves be a reverse form of recognition. They show he was taken seriously, even by those who misunderstood his purposes. Let us now try to understand.

Chapter 5

SCHWEITZER AS A RELIGIOUS LIBERAL

Dr. Schweitzer told Charles Joy and Homer Jack that in Europe he was supported by Catholics and in the United States by Protestants, but that it was the Unitarians who supported him in both Europe and America. What is the background of the religious attitudes of and toward the famed doctor-theologian-philosopher-musician?

When, in the years following the end of World War II, the question of Schweitzer's Christianity was raised, many thought the issue was a new discovery, a new trial, a new challenge. Actually, it was the old, proverbial controversy that perennially surrounded "le grand Docteur." In 1948 the English literary critic, John Middleton Murry, published a short work in London entitled *The Challenge of Schweitzer,*[1] in which he said that Schweitzer was not the great exemplar of Christianity. That an American magazine would publicize the title of "the greatest soul in Christendom" as newsworthy seemed to him irresponsible. Murry saw Schweitzer as anathema to the institution of Christianity. He thought that Schweitzer denied too many sacred Christian doctrines to be even allowed in the door, let alone called "the greatest soul in Christendom." Schweitzer denied, for instance, the divinity of Christ, the Immaculate Conception, the miracles, atonement, the supremacy of faith, and the inerrancy of the Scriptures as presenting the total revelation of God. No man who did this was rightly a Christian.

[1] J. Middleton Murry, *The Challenge of Schweitzer,* London, Jason, 1948.

A noted English churchman and biographer of Schweitzer, Dr. George Seaver, answered this *Challenge* in 1951 with his short book, *Albert Schweitzer: A Vindication,*[2] which seemed to many to show Dr. Schweitzer in perspective as a rational Christian, one who was, theologically, a liberal, yet in an ethical sense a Christian. The argument did not end here. Schweitzer was awarded the 1952 Nobel Peace Prize and the controversy concerning his Christianity errupted in the Scandinavian countries. This led, most notably, to the publication of the study by the Norwegian psychiatrist, Dr. Gabriel Langfeldt, *Albert Schweitzer: A Study of His Philosophy of Life.*[3]

Gabriel Langfeldt's book, written originally in Norwegian, specifically approached the question of whether or not Dr. Schweitzer was Christian. It may be pointed out that Dr. Schweitzer did not accept the traditional concepts of God, prayer, the supremacy of faith over reason, the deity of Christ, the sacraments, the Virgin Birth, atonement, resurrection, or ascension. Both Mr. Murry and Mr. Langfeldt catalog these heresies. Dr. Langfeldt, however, an admirer of Schweitzer, goes on to deal sympathetically with the question of Schweitzer's relationship to Christianity. He quotes a venerable Scandinavian bishop as saying it is "a disgrace that the question has ever been raised" concerning Schweitzer's Christianity, in view of his practical application of the ethics of Christianity. This basically is Dr. Langfeldt's position. He ends by answering the question, "Is he a Christian?", saying " 'No,' if you mean in a doctrinal sense, but 'yes' if you mean in terms of conduct and character." The studied arguments carefully developed by Messrs. Murry, Seaver and Langfeldt may be followed by those interested in this pursuit.

A noted American professor, Dr. Walter M. Horton—retired from Oberlin College and more recently at the Sorbonne—touches on this question. His approach is shown in his book, *Contemporary Continental Theology,*[4] in which, under the

2 George Seaver, *Albert Schweitzer: A Vindication,* Boston, Beacon, 1951.

3 Gabriel Langfeldt, *Albert Schweitzer: A Study of his Philosophy of Life,* New York, Braziller, 1960.

4 Walter Horton, *Contemporary Continental Theology,* New York, Harper, 1938, pp. 194-195.

section on French Thought, he discusses Schweitzer in these terms:

> I do not want to give the impression that liberal theology in France is altogether mute and apologetic, or on the defensive. . . . There is one unabashed and unrepentant liberal in France who would give the lie to any such assertion: Albert Schweitzer. Whether he is really a Frenchman or a citizen of the world is a bit problematic. . . . But whether he is a Frenchman or not, there is no doubt that Schweitzer is a liberal. Others have drawn conservative conclusions from his studies in the eschatology of the New Testament. . . . Schweitzer has never subscribed to these conclusions. Though he promised the mission board to be "dumb as a carp" on theological questions if they would consent to send him to Africa, he has never been hesitant about expressing his heresies in print. Frankly, he believes that Jesus and Paul were entirely mistaken in their eschatology. What we moderns must do, he believes, is "take the ethical religion of Jesus out of the setting of his world-view and put it in our own," and thus under the influence of the spirit of his ethical religion, to "make the kingdom of God a reality in this world by works of love."

Dr. Schweitzer in his autobiographical writings clearly denoted the development from his earliest youth of his break with orthodoxy as he found it around him. He could not accept the prayers of childhood because they pertained only to humans and not to animals and other life. Consequently, he tells us that he made his own addition to the prayers taught him.

He felt compassion belonged to all life, and out of this developed later his ethical "Reverence for Life."

In his description of his preparation for confirmation in the Lutheran Church he found himself at odds with the passages he had to affirm so that he had to "keep myself closely shut up," adding, "My ideas differed from his [Pastor Wennagel's] in spite of all the respect I showed him." Then follows Schweitzer's rather famous passage on thinking as primary to religion. He said: "He [Pastor Wennagel] wanted to make us understand that in submission to faith all reasoning must be silenced. But I was convinced—and I am so still—that the fundamental principles of Christianity have to be proved true by reasoning, and by no other method. Reason, I said to myself, is given us that we may bring everything within the range of its action, even the most exalted ideas of religion. And this certainly filled me with joy."[5]

When he grew up, Dr. Schweitzer, like others before him, was moved to try and make meaningful the ethics of Jesus by actually practicing them. His early effort to found a society for the aiding of paroled prisoners is one such example. His later decision to go to Africa, giving up the acclaim, comfort and position already acquired in Europe and undertaking the arduous task of returning to college to receive an entirely different type of education in order to become a medical doctor, is well known. He relates what prompted such a decision:

> One morning in the autumn of 1904 I found on my writing table in the college one of the green-covered magazines in which the Paris Missionary Society reported every month on its activities. A certain Miss Scherdlin used to put them there knowing that I was specially interested in this society on account of the impression made on me by the letters of one of its earliest missionaries, Casalis by name, when my father read them aloud at his missionary services during my childhood. That evening, in the very act of putting it aside that I might go on with my work I mechanically opened this magazine, which had been laid on my table during my absence. As I did so, my eye caught the title of an article: "Les Besoins de la Mission du Congo" (The Needs of the Congo Mission).
>
> It was by Alfred Boegner, the president of the Paris Missionary Society, an Alsatian, and contained a complaint that the mission had not enough workers to carry on its work in the Gabon, the northern province of the Congo Colony. The writer expressed his hope that his appeal

[5] *Memoirs of Childhood and Youth,* p. 43.

would bring some of those "on whom the Master's eyes already rested" to a decision to offer themselves for this urgent work. The conclusion ran: "Men and women who can reply simply to the Master's call, 'Lord, I am coming,' those are the people whom the Church needs." Having finished the article, I quietly began my work. My search was over.

My thirtieth birthday a few months later I spent like the man in the parable who "desiring to build a tower, first counts the cost whether he have wherewith to complete it." The result was that I resolved to realize my plan of direct human service in Equatorial Africa. . . .

What seemed to my friends the most irrational thing in my plan was that I wanted to go to Africa, not as a missionary, but as a doctor, and thus when already thirty years of age burdened myself, as a beginning, with a long period of laborious study. And that this study would mean for me a tremendous effort, I had no manner of doubt. I did, in truth, look forward to the next few years with dread. But the reasons which determined me to follow the way of service I had chosen, as a doctor, weighed so heavily that other considerations were as dust in the balance. . . .

I wanted to be a doctor that I might be able to work without having to talk. For years I had been giving myself out in words and it was with joy that I had followed the calling of theological teacher and of preacher. But this new form of activity I could not represent to myself as being talking about the religion of love, but only as an actual putting it into practice. Medical knowledge made it possible for me to carry out my intention in the best and most complete way, wherever the path of service might lead me. In view of the plan for Equatorial Africa, the acquisition of such knowledge was especially indicated because in the district to which I thought of going a doctor was, according to the missionaries' reports, the most needed of all needed things. They were always complaining in their magazine that the natives who visited them in physical suffering could not be given the help they desired. To become one day the doctor whom these poor creatures needed, it was worthwhile, so I judged, to become a medical student. Whenever I was inclined to feel that the years I should have to sacrifice were too long, I reminded myself that Hamilcar and Hannibal had prepared for their march on Rome by their slow and tedious conquest of Spain.

There was still one more point of view from which I seemed directed to become a doctor. From what I knew of the Parisian Missionary Society, I could not but feel it to be very doubtful whether they would accept me as a missionary.[6]

But there is further amplification of his need to go to Africa. Norman Cousins supplies this in *Dr. Schweitzer of Lambarene.* He gives us this explanation in Schweitzer's own words:

'As a young man, my main ambition was to be a good minister', he explained. 'I completed my studies; then, after a while I started to teach. I became the principal of the seminary. All this while I had been studying and thinking about the life of Jesus and the meaning of Jesus. And the more I studied and thought, the more convinced I became that Christian theology had become over-complicated. In the early centuries after Christ, the beautiful simplicities relating to Jesus became somewhat obscured by the conflicting interpretations and the incredibly involved dogma growing out of the theological debates. For example, more than a century after Christ, there was a theological dispute growing out of questions such as these:

'Is Jesus actually God or the son of God?

'If he is God, why did he suffer? If he was the son of God, why was he made to suffer?

'What is meant by the spirit of Jesus?

'What is the true position of Mary in Christian theology?

'Elaborate theology dealing with such questions disturbed me, for it tended to lead away from the great and simple truths revealed in Jesus' own words and life. Jesus Christ did proclaim himself to be God or the son of God; his mission was to awaken people to the Kingdom of God which he felt to be imminent.

'In my effort to get away from intricate Christian theology based on later interpretations, I developed some ideas of my own. These ideas were at variance with the ideas that

[6] *Out of My Life and Thought,* pp. 107, 114-15.

had been taught me. Now, what was I to do? Was I to teach that which I myself had been taught but that I now did not believe? How could I, as the principal of a seminary, accept the responsibility for teaching young men that which I did not believe?

'But was I to teach that which I did believe? If I did so, would this not bring pain to those who had taught me?

'Faced with these two questions, I decided that I would do neither. I decided that I would leave the seminary. Instead of trying to get acceptance for my ideas, involving painful controversy, I decided I would make my life my argument, I would advocate the things I believed in terms of the life I lived and what I did. Instead of vocalizing my belief in the existence of God within each of us, I would attempt to have my life and work say what I believed.'[7]

Here, in this passage, we see the heretic and dissenter who must move on.

Dr. Schweitzer's religious liberalism was already well known. In a conversation we had in 1962 he told me that at the time he was ordained by the synod in Strasbourg he knew there was probably not another synod of the Lutheran church that would have done so because of the heresies he had already put into print.

His studies of the historical Jesus led him further and further away from orthodox Christianity and closer to the position of the religious liberal. Concerning those studies, he wrote: "The satisfaction which I could not help feeling at having solved so many historical riddles about the existence of Jesus was accompanied by the painful consciousness that this new knowledge in the realm of history would mean unrest and difficulty for Christian piety."[8]

This sense of having upset the piety of other Christians by his scholarly research troubled him deeply and helps explain his decision not to stand and make an issue but to go forth and demonstrate his faith in terms of action.

[7] Norman Cousins, *Dr. Schweitzer of Lambarene,* New York, Harper, 1960, pp. 190-91.

[8] *Out of My Life and Thought,* p. 65. See also Chapter VI, entire, and Chapter XII, particularly pp. 141-154.

He had not seen the last of this difficulty, however; it was to plague him for years, indeed for decades. His writings continued to clarify the growing liberalization of thought represented by his studies of the New Testament, comparative religions, and the relationship of religion to contemporary culture. He saw that the congealed institutionalism of religion was immobilized.

He found orthodox Christians not ready to "go the second mile" in putting to practical test the ethical principles of Jesus of Nazareth. To him this demand was an all-consuming summons. He had tried to "devote myself to tramps and discharged prisoners." With Rev. Augustus Ernst, an undertaking was carried forward which prepared him for his later service, although he himself felt it taught more by what was not accomplished rather than by what was. "In our youthful inexperience we no doubt often failed. . . ."[9] But from it he was prepared for what came afterward.

Then, after this "foolhardy undertaking" came his announcement of his plan to go to Africa:

> 'My relatives and friends all joined in expostulating with me on the folly of my enterprise. I was a man, they said, who was burying the talent entrusted to him. . . .
>
> 'In the many verbal duels which I had to fight, as a weary opponent, with people who passed for Christians, it moved me strangely to see them so far from perceiving that the effort to practice the love preached by Jesus may sweep a man into a new course of life, . . . I had assumed as a matter of course that familiarity with the sayings of Jesus would produce a much better appreciation of what to popular logic is non-rational. . . .' [10]

It was not merely the pietistic and orthodox who did not comprehend the direction of his thought and his summons to ethical action. Religious liberals also found Dr. Schweitzer undermining their preconceived positions. His own words clarify this development: "The historical Jesus moves us deeply by his subordination to God. In this he stands out as

[9] *Ibid.*, p. 104.
[10] *Ibid.*, p. 108.

greater than the Christ personality of dogma which, in compliance with the claims of Greek metaphysics, is conceived as omniscient and incapable of error."[11]

This paragraph clearly marks Dr. Schweitzer as a Unitarian so far as his Christology is concerned. Obviously, also, this passage says that to be less than divine is to be "greater than the Christ personality"—as Jesus becomes a human personality, he is greater than the divine personality of historical Christianity. This was heresy for all Christians except Unitarian Universalists.

Yet, in the paragraph immediately following, Dr. Schweitzer goes on to clarify why even liberal Christians were not happy with this interpretation: "(It) was at once a heavy blow for liberal Protestantism. For generations the latter had busied itself investigating the life of Jesus in the conviction that all progress in the knowledge of history could not but make more evident that undogmatic character in the religion of Jesus."[12] Further along in this paragraph he writes: "I myself have suffered in this matter, by having had to join in the work of destroying the portrait of Christ on which liberal Christianity based its appeal. At the same time I was convinced that this liberal Christianity was not reduced to living on an historical illusion, but could equally appeal to the Jesus of history, and further, that it carried its justification in itself."[13]

Norman Cousins gives us further insight from his conversations with Dr. Schweitzer regarding his motivation to come to Africa, and its religious and intellectual background and repercussions. Thus, Mr. Cousins reported that Schweitzer told him:

> Then, after a moment, he (Schweitzer) said he did not want anyone to believe what he had done was the result of hearing the voice of God or anything like that. The decision he had made was a completely rational one, consistent with everything else in his own life.

[11] *Ibid.*, p. 72.
[12] *Ibid.*, p. 73.
[13] *Ibid.*

Indeed, he said, some theologians had told him that they had had direct word from God. He didn't argue. All he could say about that was that their ears were sharper than his.

He said, however, that he believed in the evolution of human spirituality, and that the higher this development in the individual, the greater his awareness of God. Therefore, if by the expression 'hearing the voice of God', one means a pure and lively and advanced development of spirituality, then the expression was correct. This is what is meant by the 'dictates of the spirit.'

By an advanced spiritual evolution, he emphasized that he was not thinking so much in theological terms as in ethical and moral terms.[14]

I know of no more persistent example of courage in standing for one's religious principles and singleness of purpose than that of Dr. Schweitzer's effort to be accepted as a medical doctor without sacrificing his intellectual integrity. Dr. Schweitzer's account of his travail and struggle to win acceptance is given in Chapter IX, "I Resolve to Become a Jungle Doctor," and Chapter XI, "Preparations for Africa," of his book, *Out of My Life and Thought.* I recommend these chapters for more thorough study. He writes, "It was in pietistic and orthodox circles that at the beginning of the nineteenth century societies were first formed for preaching the Gospel in the heathen world. . . . The faith that was in the fetters of dogmatism was first in the field." (Page 115). He tells us that his father thought he could detect a more liberal attitude in the Paris Missionary Society. "He particularly appreciated the fact that Casalis and others among its leading missionaries used in their reports not the sugary language of Canaan, but that of the simple Christian heart." (Page 117). He continues, "But that the question of orthodoxy played the same role in the Committee of the Paris Society as in others I at once learnt, and very explicitly, when I offered it my services. The kindly Director . . . at once confided to me

[14] Cousins, *op. cit.,* pp. 120, 192.

that serious objections would be raised to my theological standpoint." (Page 117).

The assurance on Dr. Schweitzer's part that he wanted to go "merely as a physician" cut no ice. A theological clearance was necessary. Members of the Committee did not want a doctor who had "only correct Christian love," and did not, "in their opinion, hold also the correct Christian belief." (Page 117).

He offered to go at his own expense, after having completed his medical studies and internship, and having raised funds from friends. Dr. Schweitzer related that "It was resolved to invite me to appear before the Committee and hold an examination into my beliefs. I could not agree to this." Quoting Jesus' example in asking nothing of his followers but to follow him, Dr. Schweitzer continued: "I also sent a message to the Committee that . . . a missionary society would be in the wrong if it rejected even a Mohammedan who offered his services for the treatment of their suffering natives. Not long before this the mission had refused to accept a minister who wanted to go and work for it because his scientific convictions did not allow him to answer with an unqualified 'yes' the question whether he regarded the Fourth Gospel as the work of the Apostle John. To avoid a similar fate I declined to appear before the assembled Committee and let them put theological questions to me." (Page 138).

He countered with an offer to meet each member of the Committee personally in his own home and give them a chance to know him as a person. In spite of a "chilly reception" by several members of the committee, they finally decided to allow him to go, at his own expense, if he agreed to be *"muet comme une carpe"*—as mute as a fish—on theological matters (Pages 138-139). He had previously decided that "I wanted to be a doctor that I might be able to work without having to talk. For years I had been giving myself over to words.... But this new form of activity... (was) actually putting it into practice." (Pages 114-115).

Consequently, he was more than willing to go with the understanding that he would not preach or define doctrine and faith. Such was the paradox laid upon him by the Mission Board, however, that in order to finance himself, inasmuch as the Mission Board would not, he had to write, and return to lecture, and so was forced to break his promise to be "as mute as a fish" when away from Gabon. In Gabon he followed the call for silence, but to finance himself, he could not. Thus, instead of burying himself as a physician in the jungle, he created a greater image through his necessity to be independent of the Mission Board. This is all the world's gain, most of all that of the liberal religious world, for the philosophical, ethical and religious writings of Dr. Schweitzer over the years have constantly added to the dimension of one of the world's great rational thinkers—a spokesman for liberal religion and a champion of the primacy of the ethical and moral as true religion. In addition, he has proved his faith by his life.

The Paris Mission Society, in its fear of the liberalism of Schweitzer, helped recreate the image. From 1913 until interned as a Prisoner of War in 1917, his hospital was in the Mission, but in 1924 he received his own concession from the government and became truly independent. From then on he could speak without restrictions, and, of course, always without reservations, maintaining his own integrity. Therefore, Albert Schweitzer emerges from his half century of African service as a religious liberal of universal proportion, as a Unitarian of universal dimension, and as a universal mind of comprehensive scope. Unfortunately, many people have not understood the full scope of Schweitzer's intellectual scrutiny of our institutions—religious, cultural and social—and so are shocked today to realize that Schweitzer is the type of nonconformist or dissenter he is. Nevertheless, it should be obvious that throughout the years he has been consistent.

In spite of his intellectual scrutiny of Christian institutions and doctrines, he was emotionally and ethically close to the church and to churchmen. He loved the church as an institution and appreciated its contributions to a loftier life for all mankind. He simply called upon the church to be also true to a higher standard of private and public morals: intellectual honesty, the truth, and the spirit of the inquiring mind. Only thus can its morality be maintained, he believed. Thus, he did not see himself as attacking the church, but as urging it to self-improvement.

Part of the quandary of Schweitzer, too, was that he not only attacked church doctrines but also expressed some of the most noble sentiments on behalf of broader church toleration. In our day, when interfaith understanding and ecumenism are emphasized, we find in Schweitzer's books ennobling thoughts of the ecumenical spirit at work in the life of one man. He gives us precious accounts of his Protestant love of the Catholic church and his esteem for the beauty of its form and the faithfulness of its adherents. When he first went to Africa in 1913 he wrote a memorable sentence in the opening pages of *On the Edge of the Primeval Forest*: "It was, and is still, my conviction that the humanitarian work to be done in the world should, for its accomplishment, call upon us as men, not as members of any particular nation or religious body." Dr. Schweitzer was one of the first great exponents in our century of the principle of people acting and dealing with one another as human beings, rather than as members of a particular group. He was one of the first great universal minds—those unable to extend their loyalties to those who are different may find it hard to accept his broadminded sympathies.

In the numerous memoirs of Dr. Schweitzer, there is one paragraph that stands out. He spent three difficult years as a Prisoner of War in Africa. Under house arrest at first, he was later allowed to resume management of the hospital and to visit regularly both the Catholic and Protestant missions. Word came of his internment and deportation. He was taken aboard the river steamer, and gives us this recollection: "Just as we had been taken on board the river steamer and the natives were shouting to us an affectionate farewell from the bank, the Father Superior of the Catholic Mission came on board, waved aside with an authoritative gesture the native soldiers who tried to prevent his approach, and shook hands with us: 'You shall not leave the country,' he said, 'without my thanking you both [Mrs. Schweitzer was with him] for all the good you have done it.' We were never to see each other again. Shortly after the war he lost his life on board the *Afrique,* the ship which took us to Europe, when she was wrecked in the Bay of Biscay."[15]

In his summary of his first sojourn in Africa, Dr. Schweitzer writes this description: "The most difficult problem in the mission field arises from the fact that the evangelistic work has to be done under two banners, the Catholic and the Protestant. How much grander would be the work undertaken in the name of Jesus if this distinction did not exist and there were never two churches working in competition. On the Ogowe, indeed, the missionaries of both bodies live in quite correct, sometimes in friendly, relations with one another, but that does not remove the rivalry which confuses the native and hinders the spread of the Gospel. I often visit the Catholic mission stations in my capacity of doctor and so have been able to gather a fairly clear idea of the way in which they conduct their evangelistic work and education."[16]

Of course, the Doctor's whole life had prepared him for rising above the wall of bigotry which prevents most people from seeing other religious groups with equality, and as men and women. In his *Memoirs of Childhood and Youth* he gives us these recollections of the wider loyalty of Catholic and Protestant. Writing long before the existence of the Ecumenical Council, with its new spirit of church unity and harmony, Dr. Schweitzer spoke for understanding. No wonder he is often looked upon as a Protestant maverick, for he was truly an ecumenical person. He recalled:

> In the homesick longing which I felt at Mülhausen for the Günsbach Sunday, the actual building in which we worshipped played a part. The fine new Mülhausen church struck me as terribly defective, because it had no chancel. In the church at Günsbach my devotional dreams could expand and be enriched in a Catholic chancel, for the church—as I will explain—was used for their services by Catholics and Protestants alike.

[15] *Out of My Life and Thought,* p. 194.
[16] *On the Edge of the Primeval Forest,* pp. 111-12.

When Alsace during the reign of Louis Quatorze (1643-1715) became French, that monarch, wishing to humiliate the Protestants, decreed that in every Protestant village in which there was a minority of at least seven Catholic families the chancel of the church should be given up for their exclusive use. The whole building was also to be at their disposal for services every Sunday at fixed times. Thus it came about that a number of churches in Alsace are Protestant and Catholic at the same time. In the second half of the nineteenth century the number of such churches became somewhat smaller, because many parishes decided to have a separate church built for the Catholics, but at Günsbach, as in many other places, this joint use of the one building by both confessions has remained to the present day.

The Catholic chancel, into which I used to gaze, was to my childish imagination the *ne plus ultra* of magnificence. There was first an altar painted to look like gold, with huge bunches of artificial flowers upon it; then tall candlesticks of metal with majestic wax candles in them; on the wall, above the altar and between the two windows, was a pair of large gilt statues, which to me were Joseph and the Virgin Mary; and all these objects were flooded with the light which came through the chancel windows. Then through the windows themselves one looked out over trees, roofs, clouds, and blue sky on a world, in short, which continued the chancel of the church into an infinity of distance, and was, in its turn, flooded with a kind of transfiguring glory imparted to it by the chancel. Thus my gaze wandered from the finite to the infinite, and my soul was wrapped in peace and quiet. . . .

One thing more I have taken with me into life from this little church, that was Protestant and Catholic at the same time, I mean religious tolerance. These Catholic-Protestant churches, which had their origin in the irresponsible edict of a ruler, are for me something more than a historical phenomenon. They are a symbol to show that the differences which separate churches today are things which are destined ultimately to disappear. When I was still merely a child, I felt it to be something beautiful that in our village Catholics and Protestants worshipped in the same building, and my heart fills with joy today whenever I set foot inside it. I should like all the churches in Alsace which are still used by both confessions to remain so, as a prophecy of, and an exhortation to, a future of religious unity, upon which we must ever keep our thought fixed if we are really and truly Christians. . . .

My grandfather Schillinger, whom I never knew, had been an enthusiast for the Enlightenment; he was filled with the spirit of the eighteenth century. After service he used to tell the people, who waited for him in the street, the political news, and also make them acquainted with the latest discoveries of the human mind. If there was anything special to be seen in the sky, he would in the evening set up his telescope in front of the house and let anyone who liked look through it.

As the Catholic vicar was also under the influence of the spirit of the eighteenth century, and its tolerance, the two ministers lived in their respective residences in brotherly union. If one had more visitors than he could take in, he found a bed for one in the other house. If one went off for a holiday, it followed that the other visited the sick members of his congregation in order that they might not be left without any spiritual ministrations. When on Easter morning the Catholic vicar had finished his Masses and went home for a good Easter meal, my grandfather would open his window and wish him joy at having reached the end of his fast.

One night there was a big fire in the village. As the evangelical manse seemed threatened, they brought its contents out and housed them in the vicarage, whereby it happened that my grandmother's crinolines got set up in the Catholic vicar's bedroom, and were brought from there back into the manse the next morning.[17]

In consequence, whichever way we look at Schweitzer's religious background we see the individualist, in some ways too challenging, in some ways too broadminded, and in some ways too harmonious with all religious groups, to develop the united and undivided loyalties of any one group. As has been said over the years, whether he is a Christian in doctrinal matters or not, he is a Christian in the broader sense of his

[17] *Memoirs of Childhood and Youth,* pp. 41-42, 76-78, 79-80.

spirit of gracious acceptance, kindly trust and human love for all his fellows, human and non-human. No wonder Father John O'Brien wrote appreciatively of him in the *Reader's Digest* some years ago as "God's eager fool," and Pope Paul eulogized him at the opening of the third session of the Vatican Council in September, 1965.

Chapter 6

THE PRISONER OF PEACE

The Christian Century magazine, in its issue of November 21, 1934, gave Dr. Schweitzer's summary of his Hibbert Lectures delivered at Manchester College, Oxford, England where he spoke on *Religion in Modern Civilization.* The opening paragraph reads as follows:

> I am going to discuss religion in the spiritual life and civilization of our time. The first question to be faced, therefore, is: Is religion a force in the spiritual life of our age? I answer in your name, and mine, 'No!' . . . There is (however) a longing for religion among many who no longer belong to the churches. I rejoice to concede this. And yet we must hold fast to the fact that religion is not a force. The proof? The war . . .

This reflects the pessimism of Dr. Schweitzer before World War II. To him war was always like a storm cloud that hangs over the horizon of the mind, its dark shadows lurking over the steeples of churches and temples the world around. How can one go serenely along uncommitted to the necessity of removing war from human society? Dr. Schweitzer faced honestly the need for civilized men and modern society to recognize the ultimate alternatives of war or peace, of destruction or survival.

Dr. Schweitzer's attitude was clearly stated in 1934. While in England, he determined not to enter Nazi Germany. Hitler represented the glorified war spirit and was already embarked upon making Germany a military fortress. While lecturing in

England, Schweitzer began to receive letters from German friends who wrote to the effect: "Do not visit me when you come to Germany. I dare not speak out or take sides, and I cannot afford to risk my political neutralism or bring my thought under question." Particularly dismaying to Dr. Schweitzer was the increasing number of church leaders and pastors in the state church who wrote in this vein. Thus, he was led to his conclusion that a state-connected church cannot be "the plumb line to God" (Amos 7) in the hour of social and national moral failure. Accordingly, Dr. Schweitzer cancelled his previously scheduled speaking dates and concerts in Germany and never set foot in Germany as long as Hitler lived.

Dr. Schweitzer thought back to these days when the Hamburg publisher, Rowholt Verlag, sent him a copy of Rolf Hochhuth's play *The Deputy*. On June 30, 1963, Dr. Schweitzer wrote the publishers: "I was an active witness to the failure which took place in those days, and I believe we must concern ourselves with this great problem of the events of history. We owe this to ourselves, for our failure made us all participants in the guilt of those days. After all, the failure was not that of the Catholic Church alone, but that of the Protestant Church as well.The Catholic Church bears the greater guilt, for it was an organized, supra-national power in a position to do something, whereas the Protestant Church was an unorganized, impotent, national power. But it, too, became guilty by simply accepting the terrible inhuman fact of the persecution of the Jews." The two attitudes which stand out are clear; his own Protestant church had shown itself to be "an unorganized, impotent, national power"; and the guilt of silence – of not speaking up – must be shared by all. The crime of silence should never again be allowed to be our lot. We must speak.

Yet the churches were silent. The churches of Europe, which are supported by the state, became agencies of the state. They lost their ethical tongue, and they had neither the will nor the courage to resist the popular opinion created by national pro-

1 See Rolf Hochhuth, *The Deputy,* New York, Grove, 1964, Preface.

paganda. Churches committed to following the Prince of Peace became the marshaling agencies of the spirit of war. They earned their state subsidies, but they lost their own integrity in the process. Dr. Schweitzer was utterly disillusioned by this.

World War II was more terrible than any war before. Dr. Schweitzer has given us an account of the difficult war period through which he and the hospital went. However, he was not imprisoned this time, as he had been during the previous world war. But his supplies were cut off and stringent economies were introduced. All but the most severe cases among the patients were sent home.

The Vichy French and the Free French were fighting in Africa. Battles raged along the Ogowe, particularly in the air. Since both sides agreed to respect the hospital, it was never bombed or strafed, but stray bullets and ricochets struck the hospital buildings facing the Ogowe. These buildings were all reinforced with corrugated iron previously purchased for new roofs. The war-wounded from both sides were treated in the hospital by Dr. Schweitzer. Finally, the Free French forces of General Charles de Gaulle were victorious. The *Brazza*, the African packet steamer on which Dr. Schweitzer had made his recent trips from Port Gentile to Bordeaux, was torpedoed on her return voyage to Europe. Many of his friends from Gabon were passengers, and none were saved.

After the Free French victory, the colony cooperated with the Allies. American friends of Dr. Schweitzer realized the predicament of the hospital without supplies from Europe, and formed a group, The Albert Schweitzer Fellowship, which wrote and asked what medical supplies he needed. He reported it in this way:

> At the end of the year 1940, I had a splendid surprise. Word came from America that drugs and other things would be sent to me if I would say what I needed. It was over a year before the consignment finally arrived in May, 1942. The new drugs came just in the nick of time, for our supply was nearly used up. And there were not only drugs in the

boxes, but also many other useful articles. Again and again while unpacking, shouts of joy resounded when we came across something which we especially needed. Of particular value were rubber gloves which fitted my hands. For months I had been obliged, when operating, to wear gloves too small for me. Those who had charge of the kitchen were in ecstasies over new cooking utensils. Later shipments supplemented this first one and replenished our stock. Shoes and spectacles received in 1943 were a great boon to us.

> The donations received in 1941 were just sufficient to keep things going after a fashion, but what we received in 1942 and 1943 allowed us gradually to admit more patients. How grateful I am to faithful friends in the countries that have helped me, for now I can take in all the sick who are in great need. We are greatly encouraged in our work! [2]

From this time forward, American interest and support in the Schweitzer hospital has never faltered. The Schweitzer Fellowship in New York, the Friends of Albert Schweitzer in Boston, The Albert Schweitzer Foundation in Chicago, and several West Coast Schweitzer Fellowships, among others, have all aided his hospital as their primary work. The Unitarian Service Committee made support of the Schweitzer Hospital a major non-sectarian humanitarian program during the war years. Great foundations, pharmaceutical houses, medical societies, and guilds of organists, have also given support and assistance to the hospital.

Dr. Schweitzer reflected upon the war experience and what it meant to humanity in broad ethical, cultural and philosophical terms. He thought back to the terrible experiences of World War I and to his realization then that man's ethics began and ended with man. There was, he now concluded, no basis for consistency in man's ethics, even with his fellowman. On a journey up the Ogowe to N'Gomo on an errand of mercy in 1915, he covered page after page with disconnected notes. Recalling that trip, he wrote: "Slowly we crept upstream laboriously feeling — it was the dry season — for the channels

[2] *Out of My Life and Thought,* Postscript by Everett Skillings, 1949 ed.

between the sandbanks. Lost in thought, I sat on the deck of the barge, struggling to find the elementary and universal conception of the ethical which I had not discovered in any philosophy. Late on the third day, at the very moment when, at sunset, we were making our way through a herd of hippopotami, there flashed upon my mind, unforeseen, and unsought, the phrase, 'Reverence for Life.' The iron door had yielded: the path in the thicket had become visible. Now I had found my way to the ideas in which world-and-life-affirmation and ethics are contained side by side! Now I knew that the world-view of ethical world-and life-affirmation, together with its ideals of civilization, is founded in thought."[3]

With this phrase and its attendant ideas, Dr. Schweitzer found the basis for an ethical outlook which presents a consistent philosophy that is the answer to war, destruction, violence and carnage. For the first time in Western thought, a consistent philosophy for peaceful living is offered. It is contained in the simple affirmation: "I am life which wills to live, in the midst of life which wills to live."[4] It is this will to live in the midst of will-to-life that should lead us to reverence for all of life. There is a great chain of life from which we are not separate and from which we cannot be separated except by the death of compassion in our own minds. We must have reverence and respect for all other living things, the tiny and pathetic, the great and powerful; through compassion, sympathy, and reverence of life by life, we can overcome the hostilities and the fears which are the basis of belligerency.

Schweitzer's ethics, then, is founded on fellow-feeling for all other life and is a reflective act. He wrote: "Life affirmation is the spiritual act in which he (man) ceases to live unreflectively and begins to devote himself to his life with reverence, in order to raise it to its true value. To affirm life is to deepen, to make more inward, and to exalt the will to live."[5] As the life of thought was fundamental for Dr. Schweitzer,

[3] *Out of My Life and Thought,* p. 185.
[4] *Ibid.,* p. 186.
[5] *Ibid.,* p. 187.

and as the necessity for a rational decision must always undergird actions and responses, the necessity of grounding ethics in a thoroughly rational approach—in a reflective way—was primary.

The Church as an institution has not accepted Dr. Schweitzer's thought. He told Norman Cousins, Editor of the *Saturday Review,* that "Christian theology has found it difficult to come to terms with my thought, though Christians have not." Further on, he made this distinction:

> 'I have the feeling that the Christian theologians are reluctant to come in through the door I have tried to open. I have tried to relate Christianity to the sacredness of life. It seems to me this is a vital part of Christianity as I understand it. But the Christian theologians, many of them, confine Christianity to the human form of life. It does not seem to me to be correct. It lacks the essential universalization that I associate with Jesus. Why limit reverence for life to human form? As I say, I have tried to open the door; I hope the Christian theologians will come in.'[6]

The fullest explanation of the Reverence for Life concept is found in Dr. Schweitzer's *Civilization and Ethics,* the second volume of *The Philosophy of Civilization.* He summarizes it in this way:

> The basic principle of the moral which is a necessity of thought means, however, not only an ordering and deepening, but also a widening of the current views of good and evil. A man is truly ethical only when he obeys the compulsion to help all life which he is able to assist, and shrinks from injuring anything that lives. He does not ask how far this or that life deserves one's sympathy as being valuable, nor, beyond that, whether and to what degree it is capable of feeling. Life as such is sacred to him. He tears no leaf from a tree, plucks no flower, and takes care to crush no insect. If in summer he is working by lamplight, he prefers to keep the window shut and breathe a stuffy atmosphere rather than see one insect after another fall with singed wings upon his table.
>
> If he walks on the road after a shower and sees an earth-

6 Cousins, *op. cit.,* p. 120.

> worm which has strayed on to it, he bethinks himself that it must get dried up in the sun if it does not return soon enough to ground into which it can burrow, so he lifts it from the deadly stone surface and puts it on the grass. If he comes across an insect which has fallen into a puddle, he stops a moment in order to hold out a leaf or a stalk on which it can save itself.
>
> He is not afraid of being laughed at as sentimental. It is the fate of every truth to be a subject for laughter until it is generally recognized. Once it was considered folly to assume that men of colour were really men and ought to be treated as such, but the folly has become an accepted truth. Today it is thought to be going too far to declare that constant regard for everything that lives, down to the lowest manifestations of life, is a demand made by rational ethics. The time is coming, however, when people will be astonished that mankind needed so long a time to learn to regard thoughtless injury to life as incompatible with ethics.[7]

As a result of this passage, many people tend to limit the philosophy of Reverence for Life to a discussion of our attitudes to earthworms, mosquitoes and flowers. These are important in sketching in a fundamentally consistent attitude, which we need, to all of life. However, Dr. Schweitzer stresses in many passages the need for a selective, decision-making ability which the thinking person must utilize. Life for higher aims becomes the criterion. Lesser life, or lower life, must constantly be sacrificed for higher life—but never needlessly, heedlessly or without reverent reflection of what is being done. He wrote: "To the man who is truly ethical, all life is sacred, including that which, from the human point of view, seems lower in the scale. He makes distinctions only as each case comes before him, and under the pressure of necessity, as, for example, when it falls to him to decide which of two lives he must sacrifice in order to preserve the other."[8] In another section of *Out of My Life and Thought* he gives an illustration: "I rejoice over the new remedies for sleeping sickness which enable me to preserve life, whereas I had previously to

[7] *The Philosophy of Civilization,* pp. 310-11.
[8] *Out of My Life and Thought,* p. 271.

watch a painful disease. But every time I have under the microscope the germs which cause this disease, I cannot but reflect that I have to sacrifice this life to save another."[9]

Dr. Schweitzer also writes: "If he (man) has been touched by the ethic of Reverence for Life, he injures and destroys life only under a necessity which he cannot avoid, and never from thoughtlessness."[10] Yet in making these distinctions, he is a free moral agent even to a far greater extent than is sometimes recognized by more limited ethics. For example:

> However seriously man undertakes to abstain from killing and damaging, he cannot entirely avoid it. He is under the law of necessity, which compels him to kill and to damage both with and without his knowledge. In many ways it may happen that by slavish adherence to the commandment not to kill, compassion is less served than by breaking it. When the suffering of a living creature cannot be alleviated, it is more ethical to end its life by killing it mercifully than it is to stand aloof. It is more cruel to let domestic animals which one can no longer feed die a painful death by starvation than to give them a quick and painless end by violence. Again and again we see ourselves placed under the necessity of saving one living creature by destroying or damaging another. The principle of not-killing and not-harming must not aim at being independent, but must be the servant of, and subordinate itself to, compassion. It must therefore enter into practical discussion with reality. True reverence for morality is shown by readiness to face the difficulties contained in it.[11]

Dr. Christensen, in his book *At Work With Albert Schweitzer,* relates a winsome episode in which his wife was ruthlessly attacking, with a broom, the tropical roaches which are from an inch to an inch and three quarters long. She was "so absorbed in the excitement of the chase that she discovered only too late that Dr. Schweitzer was standing in the open doorway watching her."

[9] *Ibid.*
[10] *Ibid.,* p. 272.
[11] Schweitzer, *Indian Thought and Its Development,* pp. 83-84.

"'Poor beetles,' he said, 'They've a right to live too.'

"My wife expressed some doubt about this, and a short discussion followed which ended in a compromise; the creatures might be hunted in the room, but not molested (once swept) outside the door."[12]

This type of humorous story has often been exaggerated for the sake of making parody of Dr. Schweitzer's thought. His philosophy says man must make distinctions and not destroy life simply for the sake of destruction. In accordance with this, it was his claim that a consistent philosophy to meet the challenge of war could be developed. It is little wonder that Dr. Schweitzer emerged in the period following the Second World War as one of the great speakers and thinkers in the cause of peace.

The end of war found Dr. Schweitzer just beginning a new chapter in his life, one which grew out of the thoroughly consistent philosophy he had evolved. While sitting at his desk writing some urgent letters, a white patient appeared at his window with the exciting news that the war in Europe had ended. Dr. Schweitzer wrote:

> Not until evening could I begin to think and to imagine the meaning of the end of hostilities. While the palms were gently rustling outside in the darkness, I took from its shelf my little book with the sayings of Lao-tse, the great Chinese thinker of the sixth century B.C., and read his impressive words on war and victory: "Weapons are disastrous implements, no tools for a noble being. Only when he cannot do otherwise, does he make use of them. Quiet and peace are for him the highest. He conquers, but he knows no joy in it. He who would rejoice in victory, would be rejoicing in murder. At the victory celebration, the general should take his place as is the custom at funeral ceremonies. The slaughter of human beings in great numbers should be lamented with tears of compassion. Therefore should he, who has conquered in battle bear himself as if he were at a festival of mourning."[13]

[12] Christensen, *op. cit.*, p. 63.

[13] *Out of My Life and Thought,* 1949 ed., p. 265.

Dr. Schweitzer had been a theologian, musician and philosopher. Now, as a physician, he had read a great deal of scientific literature. He had become knowledgeable in the field of chemistry, biology and physics. He became a friend of another great expatriate European, Albert Einstein. With the passing years, Dr. Schweitzer had come to think of himself as a scientist rather than as a minister, theologian or philosopher.

Charles Darwin's portrait, rather than Kant's, Goethe's, Zwingli's or Luther's, hung in his room. His perspective shifted subtly with the passing years. Contacts with medical researchers and the great foundations, and the steady and time-consuming reading of scientific papers and journals, all led to his most recent identification with the field of science. He had seen many times through his medical work that science has the power to stop suffering; this was a tangible and wonderful attribute in a world of disease and despair. How could he not affirm it? Yet through it all he still had the humanitarian sensitivity of his religious and philosophical background. He combined these with his sense of science so that he was one of those scientists who insisted that science must be humanized and deal with the practical problems of persons living, suffering, and dying in a world of imperfect choices.

Consequently, when, shortly after the explosions of the first atomic bombs on Hiroshima and Nagasaki, Dr. Schweitzer received a letter from Dr. Einstein, telling of his concern, he realized that as a scientist he must speak up. Science was not only constructive and remedial; it was destructive and deforming. Civilization hung in the balance. Inhumanity, as seen in the deaths of hundreds of thousands of people through atomic explosions, was a much more vicious means of annihilation than the conventional means of warfare. Beginning in Europe with Germany's self-propelled rockets, the personal aspect of waging war was removed. Furthermore, the incendiary bomb raids on cities made war a means of mass murder rather than a conflict between contending armies. Now, with nuclear fission, humanity was moving further along the road of the loss of value. The first reports from Hiroshima, dealing with nuclear burns and the damage to cell and tissue life, were appalling. As a scientist and humanitarian, as a thinker and a moralist, Schweitzer was compelled to enter the arena of public controversy. No ivory tower, no cloistered mission, no jungle hospital could any longer contain him. A strong stand on a controversial public issue would fracture the unanimity of support he had received, but conscience would not allow him to remain silent.

He began, as he always had, by reading and study. No partial knowledge would do for him; no half-truths would he countenance. He also began writing and receiving letters from key thinkers in the world of science and public opinion. Not only Albert Einstein, but Bertrand Russell, Linus Pauling, Dag Hammarskjold, Adlai Stevenson, Aneurin Bevan, and a host of editors, writers, scientists, ministers and molders of opinion began to correspond with him.

On November 4, 1954, when Dr. Schweitzer was the recipient of the Nobel Peace Prize in Oslo, Norway, he said:

> I know quite well that when I speak on the subject of peace, I do not contribute anything that is essentially new. My profound conviction is that the solution consists in our rejecting war for an ethical reason, because it makes us capable of inhuman crimes. Erasmus of Rotterdam, and several others after him, proclaimed this as the truth which must be followed.
>
> The only originality which I claim for myself is that in me this truth is accompanied by the certainty, born of thought, that the spirit is—in our age—capable of creating a new mentality, an ethical mentality. Inspired by such a conviction, I proclaim the truth, in the hope that my testimony can contribute to the recognition that it has validity not only in words but in practice. More than one truth has remained totally, or for a long time, without effect simply because nobody envisaged that it could become a reality.

He continued in this notable address to point out that the absence of peace does not negate the peace idea: nations still feel menaced and the right of self-defense is demanded by all; yet the hope for peace burns on in the hearts of people and in the institutions created to foster it. "In the name of all who work for peace, I beg the nations to take the first step on this new way."[14]

Here is summed up his optimism: that in spite of all the potential damages and dangers, there is the potential and the living option "in the certainty" that in our day we are "capable of creating a new mentality, an ethical mentality." This hope and belief in the possibility of creating an ethical mentality is his affirmative contribution to social thought in the present-day world.

Yet while Dr. Schweitzer was optimistic that the present generation is capable of taking this step in our day, he was pessimistic about the state of current social, political and intellectual attitudes that should lead the way. There is, in his judgment, an atmosphere of apathy and gloom. People feel there is no need for the individual's commitment; the individual resigns himself, believing nothing can be done to halt the stockpiling and preparations for nuclear extermination. The issue is too big for a single man to confront, and so he turns aside to avoid it. Therefore, no effort is made by the ethical and moral person, and the few voices heard are not taken seriously.

Albert Einstein died in despair of a broken heart. "Why won't they listen? Why won't they listen?" he said over and over before his death. From his old friend, these words of despair were a clarion call for the world to listen to. Dag Hammarskjold was despondent and fearful for the future just before his plane crashed in Africa, Dr. Schweitzer reported. In addition, the failure of the churches, the silence of writers and editors who knew the danger, and the timidity of statesmen and political leaders who dared not tell the people the sober truth—that armament and preparedness will lead to disaster—increased the despair felt by Dr. Schweitzer.

[14] Nobel Peace Prize Address, Oslo, November 4, 1954. Complete text pub. by Harper & Bros., 1955, and in the *Christian Register,* Unitarian, 25 Beacon St., Boston, January 1955.

The Paris-based news commentator, Bernard Redmont, interviewed Dr. Schweitzer after the award of the Nobel Peace Prize. Mr. Redmont asked Dr. Schweitzer what one man could do to advance Reverence for Life.

"Just do what you can," Dr. Schweitzer replied, "It's not enough merely to exist. It's not enough to say, 'I'm earning enough to live and support my family. I do my work well. I am a good father. I'm a good husband. I'm a good churchgoer.' That's all very well, but you must do something more. Seek always to do some good somewhere. Every man has to seek in his own way to make his own self more noble and to realize his true worth. You must give some time to your fellow man. Even if it's a little thing, do something for those who have need of man's help, something for which you get no pay but the privilege of doing it. For remember, you don't live in a world all your own. Your brothers are here, too."[15]

Just as each person must do what he can, so each must speak out on behalf of peace. To Dr. Schweitzer it is as elemental as that. Only as numerous individuals take a stand and make their news editors, church leaders, and political leaders know their feelings, can the moral sensibility of the world be mobilized against the practical-minded approach which inevitably prevents war by starting war.

Dr. Schweitzer remained an idealist, but he was a tough-minded one. The protest against the H-bomb, he wrote on April 14, 1954, to the London *Daily Herald,* should be started by the scientists. "If they all raised their voices, each one feeling himself impelled to tell the terrible truth, they would be listened to, for then humanity would understand that the issues were grave. . . . But the scientists must speak up. Only they have the authority to state that we can no longer take upon ourselves the responsibility for these experiments, only they can say it. There you have my opinion. I give it to you with anguish in my heart, anguish which holds me from day to day."

Later, in a series of three radio addresses broadcast from

[15] *This Week* Magazine, New York, "Words to Live By," November 29, 1959.

Oslo, Norway on April 28, 29 and 30, 1958, Dr. Schweitzer again spoke up.[16] He makes clear the potential harm of radioactivity. He explains:

> The radioactive elements released in the air by nuclear tests do not stay there permanently. In the form of radioactive rain and radioactive snow, they fall down on the earth. They enter the plants through leaves and roots and stay there. We absorb them through the plants by drinking milk from the cows or by eating the meat of animals which have fed on them. Radioactive rain infects our drinking water.
>
> The most powerful radioactive poisoning occurs in the areas between the Northern latitudes 10° and 60° because of the numerous nuclear tests conducted mainly in these latitudes by the Soviet Union and the United States.
>
> The radioactive elements absorbed over the years by our bodies are not evenly distributed in the cellular tissue, but are deposited and accumulated at certain points. From these points the internal radiation takes place, causing injuries to particularly vulnerable organs. What this kind of radiation lacks in strength is made up for by its persistence, working as it does day and night for years.
>
> It is a well-known fact that one of the most widespread and dangerous elements absorbed by us is Strontium 90. It is stored in the bones and from there emits its rays into cells of red bone marrow, where the red and white corpuscles are made. Blood diseases—fatal in most cases— are the result. The cells of the reproductive organs are particularly sensitive to this element. Even relatively weak radiation may lead to fatal consequences.
>
> The most sinister aspect of both internal and external radiation is that years may pass before the evil consequences appear. Indeed, they make themselves felt, not in the first generation, but in the following ones. Generation after generation, for centuries to come, will witness the birth of an ever-increasing number of children with mental and physical defects.[17]

The scientist is still a moralist. He cannot comprehend how

[16] Schweitzer, *Peace or Atomic War?*
[17] *Ibid.*, pp. 14-15.

we can accept the responsibility for stunting the growth of future generations. He writes of "the complete disregard of their harmful effects on future generations which, according to the biologists and physicians, will be the result of the radiation to which we are being exposed."[18] Then the physician, the family doctor in him speaks: "Only those who have never been present at the birth of a deformed baby, never witnessed the despair of its mother, dare to maintain that the risk in going on with nuclear tests is one which must be taken under existing circumstances."[19] He quoted the renowned French biologist and geneticist, Jean Rostand, who called the continuation of nuclear testing *"le crime dans l'avenir"* (the crime projected into the future).

In personal conversations Dr. Schweitzer stressed: "It is as a scientist, not as a theologian, that I speak. As a physician and biologist, I am concerned about the physical damage to the hereditary genes of future generations."

Also, his natural sense of fairness was often expressed. In one of the Oslo radio addresses he noted: "It is strange that so far nobody has stressed that the question of whether nuclear tests should be stopped or continued is not one which concerns the nuclear powers exclusively. Who is giving these countries the right to experiment, in time of peace, with weapons involving serious risks for the whole world?"[20]

He began his conclusion of the first address with this emphasis: "It is high time to realize that the question of continuing or ceasing nuclear tests is an urgent matter for international law. Mankind is imperiled by the tests. Mankind insists that they stop, and has every right to do so."[21]

In the second address, he faced the issue of the danger of atomic war and all other types of modern warfare. He said:

> War no longer depends on the ability of mighty airplanes to carry bombs to their targets. Now there are guided rockets that can be launched from their starting point and

18, 19 *Ibid.*, p. 17.
20 *Ibid.*
21 *Ibid.*

> directed with accuracy to a distant target. Missiles are carried by such rockets propelled by a fuel which is constantly being developed in efficiency. The missile carried by the rocket can be an ordinary missile or one which contains a uranium warhead or an H-bomb warhead.
>
> It is said that the Soviet Union has rockets with a range of up to 625 miles, and with a probable range of up to 1,100 miles.
>
> The United States is said to possess rockets with a range of 1,500 miles.
>
> Whether the so-called intercontinental missile with a range of 5,000 miles exists cannot be ascertained. It is assumed that the problem of its production is on the way to being solved, and both East and West are occupied with its production.
>
> Although an intercontinental rocket is not yet known to be completed, America has to be prepared for submarines shooting such a projectile far into the country. These rockets proceed with immense velocity. It is expected that an intercontinental rocket would not take more than half an hour to cross the ocean with bombloads of from one to five tons.
>
> How would an atomic war be conducted today? At first the so-called local war—but today there is little difference between a local war and a global war. Rocket missiles will be used up to a range of 1,500 miles. The destruction should not be underestimated, even if caused only by a Hiroshima-type bomb, not to speak of an H-bomb.[22]

He continues to add documentation to his position from other sources. He quotes a United States general as telling a Congressional committee:

> If, at intervals of ten minutes, one hundred and ten H-bombs are dropped over the U.S.A. there would be a casualty list of about seventy million people, besides some thousands of square miles made useless for a whole generation. Countries like England, West Germany, and France could be finished off with fifteen to twenty H-bombs.[23]

[22] *Ibid.*, pp. 24-25.
[23] *Ibid.*, p. 26.

Dr. Schweitzer follows this immediately by noting:

> President Eisenhower has pointed out, after watching maneuvers under atomic attack, that defense measures in a future atomic war become useless. In these circumstances all one can do is pray.[24]

And he quotes not alone American leaders, but English:

> An English M.P. has said, with good reason, "He who uses atomic weapons becomes subject to the fate of a bee, namely, when it stings it will perish inevitably for having made use of its sting." He who uses atomic weapons to defend freedom would become subject to a similar fate.[25]

One of the regular members of Dr. Schweitzer's staff told me that Dr. Schweitzer had confided to him that he was glad when Americans came to visit him because he would have the opportunity to talk with them concerning atomic warfare. He said that in Dr. Schweitzer's judgment America holds the key to settlement, not Russia, and that if the United States would desist in making atomic weapons an instrument of national and international policy, Russia would follow suit. Although I myself had spent a number of hours talking with Dr. Schweitzer—discussing atomic warfare with him much of the time—I did not gain the impression that he felt that the full responsibility was that of the United States. In our personal discussions he often said, "Look at the world situation today! There is so much lethargy and so much apathy everywhere that one fears that the whole world might be destroyed, and yet people are unconcerned. The statesmen are unconcerned. The newspapers and writers are unconcerned. And the churches and their leaders are unconcerned. The few people who take a stand and speak out on the great questions of our time are but a tiny handful. They are hardly heard. They say Bertrand Russell is a communist and belongs in prison. Intellectuals write in their magazines, but they do not reach the

[24] *Ibid.*
[25] *Ibid.*, p. 27.

crowd and only a handful of people become concerned. When I write and speak on the question of atomic war, people in America say, 'He has become an old man who is being fooled by the communists,' and the communists say, 'He is a colonial exploiter in Africa.'" Yet in spite of his inability to arouse people from their lethargy, he continued to try.

His third address from Oslo dealt with the imperative need to negotiate. "The three nuclear powers owe it to themselves and to mankind to reach an agreement on these absolute essentials without first dealing with prior conditions." [26] He thereupon called for open meetings without secret agreements. Such summit conferences should be based, as he outlined it, upon the rights which are involved, and should be moved by the inexorable logic that calls for cessation of nuclear testing. He concluded his epic addresses by saying:

> If negotiations on disarmament are held, not as a preliminary to the renunciation of nuclear arms but as a result of it, they would have a much larger meaning. They would be a big step in the direction of finally liquidating the confused situation that followed the Second World War.
>
> Disarmament and all questions leading to a stable situation—for example, the reunification of East and West Germany—could be discussed much better after agreement had been reached on the renunciation of atomic weapons. A later conference could also deal with many issues left unsolved in the peace treaties after the Second World War.
>
> Once agreement on renunciation of nuclear arms had been reached, it would be the responsibility of the United Nations to ensure that now as in the future they would be neither made nor used. The danger that one nation or another might hit on the idea of manufacturing nuclear weapons will have to be borne in mind for some considerable time. We must consider ourselves lucky that they are not yet in the possession of other peoples in the world.
>
> The problem of how far disarmament and renunciation of all weapons can go will have to be investigated, because the Second World War showed what terrible destruction

[26] *Ibid.*, p. 40.

conventional weapons can cause, destruction which the development of rockets has potentially vastly increased. One wishes that agreement could be reached immediately to renounce rockets and missiles, but this can come only as a result of a spiritual advance everywhere which as yet it is difficult to visualize.

Of all the very difficult problems the future holds, the most difficult will be the rights of access of over-populated countries to neighboring lands. But if in our time we renounce nuclear arms we shall have taken the first step on the way to the distant goal of the end to all wars. If we do not do this we remain on the road that leads in the near future to atomic war and misery.

Those who are to meet at the Summit must be aware of this, so that they can negotiate with propriety, with an adequate degree of seriousness, and with a full sense of responsibility. The Summit Conference must not fail: mankind will not again tolerate failure. The renunciation of nuclear weapons is vital to peace.[27]

Dr. Schweitzer felt for many years that he and a few other people—scientists, professors, philosophers, churchmen, and social-minded thinkers—were speakers without an audience, voices crying into the darkness of an empty void. Then suddenly came a gleam of light. In 1962-63, the test ban negotiations in Geneva began to make progress. A giant stride forward was made when the Test Ban Treaty was agreed upon by representatives of the United States and the Soviet Union, along with other nuclear powers. Since, however, it still remained to be ratified by the governments of the world, and since Dr. Schweitzer was both hopeful and fearful, he took pen in hand and composed a letter to President John F. Kennedy (August 6, 1963). Dr. Schweitzer wrote that the treaty gave hope that "war with atomic weapons between East and West can be avoided." The press reported that Dr. Schweitzer's letter called the treaty "one of the greatest events, perhaps the greatest, in the history of the world." Dr. Schweitzer also wrote in his letter to the President that he thought of

[27] *Ibid.*, pp. 46-47.

his friend, Dr. Einstein, "with whom I joined in the fight against atomic weapons. He died in Princeton in despair. And I, thanks to your foresight and courage, am able to observe that the world has taken the first step on the road leading to peace." The White House released this letter from Hyannisport in August, following the meeting of President Kennedy's Advisory Committee on Science, which "unanimously endorsed the Nuclear Test Ban Treaty." The White House press release, after quoting Dr. Schweitzer's letter, went on to say, "The committee believes that the continued unrestricted development and exploitation of military technology by both the Soviet Union and the United States would in time lead to a net decrease in our real security."[28] This release, coming at the beginning of the critical week of debate and voting by the United States Senate, which alone has the power to make treaties, may well have been the crucial turning point for a number of senators not previously committed. Thus, from far off Lambaréné, Dr. Schweitzer's voice may have helped bring into being the Nuclear Test Ban Treaty, "one of the greatest events, perhaps the greatest, in the history of the world."

[28] This quote is from the *Washington Post-L.A. Times* story by Carroll Kilpatrick appearing in the Boston *Sunday Globe,* Sept. 1, 1963.

Chapter 7

THE OLD DOCTOR IN A NEW AFRICA

A prominent New York City minister suggested in 1961 that perhaps Dr. Schweitzer had outlived his era. Others too had wondered whether the Grand Old Man of the Ogowe was not something of an anachronism, a fossilized reminder of the early part of the century in Africa. The question of Dr. Schweitzer's relevancy in the final years of his life has to be faced in all honesty by the informed reader. Accordingly, as we consider Dr. Schweitzer in the post-World War II era, we must consider him in the light of the challenges heard.

Before doing so, another aspect of the career of Dr. Schweitzer was as one of the foremost interpreters of five people — four individuals and a collective personality. The four persons whose portraits were made clearer because of Dr. Schweitzer are Bach and Goethe of Europe, and Jesus and Paul of the ancient Near East. The fifth person is the African. We have already referred to Schweitzer's major works on the biographies of Bach and the historical Jesus. His studies into the life of St. Paul include *The Mysticism of Paul the Apostle*[1] and *Paul and His Interpreters,* together with such studies as *The Mystery of the Kingdom of God.* That we have not dealt with this creative aspect of Dr. Schweitzer's studies is not because of its lack of enduring importance.

Dr. Schweitzer presents Goethe through a series of five

[1] The Macmillan Company, New York, has published these works on Paul as well as *The Mystery of the Kingdom of God* and *The Quest of the Historical Jesus.*

memorable lectures given at different times and places. These fortunately have been translated and combined in a single volume by Charles R. Joy,[2] and are now available in an attractive paperback edition. Included is the Bicentennial Address commemorating Goethe's birth, given at Aspen, Colorado, on July 6 and 8, 1949 – the only occasion that ever brought Dr. Schweitzer to the United States.

Dr. Joy, a long time friend of Dr. Schweitzer, translator and editor of his works, as well as the co-author with Melvin Arnold of *The Africa of Albert Schweitzer,* wrote in the introduction of the Goethe lectures:

> Here, then, are two men, so much alike in many ways, so profoundly different beneath their likenesses: Goethe brilliant, self-confident, proud, autocratic; Schweitzer simple, humble, lovable, democratic. Goethe the great master of prose and poetry, and the oft erring but deeply discerning student of life; Schweitzer the great master of music and medicine, and the sublime exemplar of ethical living.[3]

These masterminds of continental culture had much in common; both were colossi; both were masters of many fields; both called universal geniuses; both had wide ranging interests; both were free minds, moderns facing the future with resolute hearts; both were commanding personalities.

Dr. Schweitzer's powers of endurance in the modern, post-World War II era was another one of his remarkable features. His physical condition and mental awareness were, until the very end, those of a man many decades younger. When he returned to Africa after World War I, his friends protested that his active life was virtually behind him and that at 47 he should settle down and stop his adventuresome traveling; but this was not for him. Later, in England, he met Sir Wilfred Grenfell, another personage with whom Dr.

[2] Beacon Press, Boston, published Schweitzer's *Goethe: Five Studies.* It also published his *The Psychiatric Study of Jesus.*

[3] Albert Schweitzer, *Goethe: Five Studies,* Boston, Beacon, 1961; Introduction by Charles R. Joy; p. 18.

Old buildings of the Hospital that President Leon MBa of Gabon has requested hospital authorities preserve as "they keep the village atmosphere which made everyone feel at home." (See Appendix.)

The author with Dr. Schweitzer, Lambaréné, 1962.

Children from the Leper Village, which was rebuilt with money from the 1952 Nobel Peace Prize.

Orphans at the Schweitzer Hospital, August, 1962.

Dr. and Mrs. Schweitzer in Lambaréné on her last trip, with one of the doctor's ever-faithful dogs. —Erica Anderson photo

Reverence for Life

Top: The Doctor offers green lettuce to goat during dry season.
Bottom: Dr. Schweitzer feeds fish to pelican whose wings had been clipped by Africans so it could not fish for itself. —Erica Anderson photo.

Patients line up twice daily to see doctors or nurses outside the pharmacy in "the Avenue of Sorrows," 1962.

Happy and well-nourished youngsters in the Schweitzer Leper Village, 1962, no longer face lives of hopeless disease as did children of leprous families throughout history.

Schweitzer had often been compared. Dr. Schweitzer reported: "We began at once to question each other about the management of our hospitals. His chief trouble was the disappearance of reindeer... mine the loss of goats... Then we burst out laughing: we were talking not as doctors concerned with patients, but as farmers concerned with livestock."[4] Some of the critics of the Schweitzer hospital would say, "See, this is what we mean: he is more concerned with the livestock and maintenance than with clinical procedure." We shall examine this criticism in a later chapter, but the experience of Dr. Grenfell corroborates Dr. Schweitzer's: that the wilderness hospital administrator must be a practical-minded man as well as a physician. That these two men could laugh at the situation showed it could be taken in stride by both.

Mrs. Charles E. B. Russell, translator of several of Schweitzer's books, wrote of him: "In British newspaper and magazine articles, I have often found him mentioned along with Livingstone and Grenfell. But without any disparagement of these two heroes, it may be said that the comparison misses one vital distinguishing point. For what was Livingstone before he went to Africa, and who was Grenfell before he went to Labrador? Whereas Schweitzer was already a very famous man in academic circles, in philosophy and theology as well as in music, when he abandoned a conspicuously successful career and everything that he loved by going to a pestilent spot on the Equator as a mere medical missionary."[5]

Others have compared Dr. Schweitzer with Mahatma Gandhi, that great Indian figure, now revered by millions, whose life also touched Africa and in whose thought and ethical conduct millions of people in Asia and elsewhere have found an inspiring example. Still others have suggested that Dr. Schweitzer was more like the great Indian poet and sage, Rabindranath Tagore. Inevitably people search for comparisons, but when all is said the fact remains that Dr. Schweitzer

[4] See 1949 ed., *Out of My Life and Thought,* p. 254.

[5] Mrs. Charles E. B. Russell, *The Path to Reconstruction,* New York, Holt, p. 6.

fitted no prototype. He was a unique personality. An American psychiatrist recently referred to Dr. Schweitzer as the outstanding example of a non-conformist in our society. Certainly he stands alone.

When Dr. Schweitzer was at Aspen, Colorado, he was called out from a banquet by a newsman anxious to complete an interview so he could meet his deadline. He wanted a more detailed explanation of what Dr. Schweitzer meant by his ethical imperative, Reverence for Life. He persisted in pressing the point, unsatisfied with Dr. Schweitzer's explanation. In the meantime, the banquet was going on and Dr. Schweitzer was getting hungry. Finally he said, "Reverence for Life means all life. I am a life. I am hungry. You should respect my rights to eat now." With that he excused himself and returned to the table.

The people at Lambaréné love the accounts that are told of his famous repartee with those fashionable women who flocked about him in Europe, putting on airs. Once, at a recital, a dowager turned to him and said, "Dr. Schweitzer, you have been in Africa for many years. Now that you are back in Europe, what are your thoughts on Western civilization?"

Dr. Schweitzer replied, "It would be a good idea!"

On another occasion, one such lady turned to him with a patronizing air and asked, "What do you do in Lambaréné for the advancement of culture?"

Dr. Schweitzer replied, "I supply slop basins to the residents of the neighborhood of Lambaréné!" This answer becomes clear when one visits Lambaréné and notes the use of the human head for carrying things. Traditionally, baskets have always been used for a "head bundle." But not now at Lambaréné, where the most popular means of carrying goods on the head is the large, flat, enamel water basin, stolen from the hospital and easily identified by the black initials "ASB" which are printed on all equipment of the Schweitzer Hospital. The "B" represents his wife's maiden name, Bresslau, used by the Doctor in connection with anything having to do with the hospital, which he looked upon as a joint venture as long as she lived.

One of the stories often told is of the friend who asked Dr. Schweitzer, the last time he was in Europe, "Why is it that you travel third class?" To which the Doctor replied, "Because there is no longer a fourth class."

Another story is often told about the time Dr. Schweitzer was to be guest of honor at a reception during one of his rare visits to Europe. He arrived at the place and was haughtily directed to the servants' entrance by the doorman. Meekly, Dr. Schweitzer obliged and found his way in to his embarrassed hostess by the back way, while the guests coming to meet him were pompously announced at the front door. To meet Dr. Schweitzer is to know how completely in character the incident is.

A friend recently showed me a letter in which a mutual acquaintance had written regarding Dr. Schweitzer: "How moving it is to find a man rather than a public figure. That for me was a religious experience, to have my hope confirmed that he had continued to do his work modestly." That fame and acclaim have not altered his humility is, indeed, a moving discovery.

Before the Doctor's death the hospital was a gathering place for many persons. In addition to the half a thousand patients treated daily, there were many visitors. The hospital became a favorite place for missionaries and other Europeans and Americans in Africa to spend a vacation. Doctors, specialists, representatives of pharmaceutical houses, inspectors for foundations, journalists, church leaders—all convene here. While efforts were made to limit the number of invitations the Doctor issued, he often found it hard to say "No" to a request. In such a setting one certainly heard conversations in three languages: English, French and German. One was occasionally startled to discover an entire conversation being conducted in a single language; but part of the remembered din and background was the confusion of languages. Then, there were also the native dialects, distinct in themselves. Consequently, this hospital has been a great international community. While I was there some older French Boy Scouts were working for the summer, and the variety of other volunteers made me realize that the Schweitzer hospital has for years been an international "Peace Corps." There were also medical interns from Germany and students from American medical schools, as well as the regularly assigned physicians. One German intern told us that he found it very difficult to work there at first because the medicine and pharmaceutical equipment were so internationalized that one needed to spend many weeks just becoming acquainted with the supplies; surgical equipment, drugs and medicine of other countries; at home he had learned the German names, but here he had to know them in English, French, Swedish and American as well.

One way in which the international character of the hospital struck me very strongly occurred during my first weekend there, when I attended a worship service held one Sunday morning. A few of the nurses were there and one or two of the doctors and interns. There were between a hundred and two hundred African adults, with as many more children and suckling babes, sitting on the ground, in the doorways, on the porches or steps, looking expectantly toward the outdoor rostrum where Dr. Walter Munz preached a sermon in French. Standing beside him were two interpreters: one Galoa, the other Fang. The preacher would read a statement without too much expression. He would then stop and one of the interpreters would step forward and give the message in the native tongue. He did so with great enthusiasm, much swinging of his arms, and great gusto, to emphasize the highlights. All of this amazed me, for he offered far more interpretation of the message than did the original speaker. Then, the second interpreter stepped forward. His method was still different. He sang the sermon, chanting at times in a loud, singsong voice. When he finished, Dr. Munz, somewhat like a professor giving a lecture, would read in a matter of fact voice his next thought. Then the native interpretations would start again. This service was at the African hospital of Dr. Schweitzer. But the doctor was not present; he was elsewhere, and I went to look for him afterward. I found him inspecting Saturday's newly poured cement foundations while the forest reverberated to the closing hymn sung in French by the uninhibited African congregation. John Gunther criticized the hospital as being the only mission in Africa he visited which was without a chapel. That this hospital is not a mission indicates how easily even gifted reporters may err in appreciating the various facets of this unique institution.[6]

Quite a different matter were the evening devotionals. These were entirely Dr. Schweitzer's services. They were held in the dining room after supper each evening. I made the following notes immediately after our first experience:

"The evening meal draws to a close. It is already dark outside, for night falls early on the equator. The white tablecloth is lighted by the kerosene lamps, with homemade dark green shades, which sit in an even row down the center of the table. Above and behind the table all is in dark shadows. As dessert is finished, uniformed members of the staff, as though by a pre-arranged signal, arise and quietly pass out ancient hymn books which they lay silently on the table.

"The low murmur of voices ceases. The last sounds of French, German and English die down. Everyone looks toward the center of the table, where Dr. Schweitzer with one massive hand picks up a book and thumbs the pages. He stops at a page, calls out the number in German, and then, rising ponderously and slowly, walks quietly around the table to the piano which is beyond him. One has the sense that he is meditating as he walks. He sits at the piano and slowly begins to improvise on its keys. He plays for a minute or two and then strikes the chord of the hymn. Remaining seated, the dinner company is instantly transformed into a congregation and joins in singing the words, which are printed in German; both tune and words, however, are familiar to all.

"From the earliest notes I was aware that this is not the famous piano with organ-pedals and zinc lining presented by the Paris Bach Society so many decades ago and to which so

[6] John Gunther, *Inside Africa,* New York, Harper, 1953; Chapter 35, "A Visit to Dr. Albert Schweitzer," p. 721 ff.

many writers have often referred. On inquiry, after the first service, I learned the famous organ-piano had long since fallen into disuse, worn out by the high humidity of the wet season and the rigorous demands of the tropical climate.

"Dr. Schweitzer rises at the conclusion of the hymn, slowly walks around the table to his place, sits himself deliberately, opens a well-thumbed Bible to a page where he has placed a storied bookmark, clears his throat, announces in German, 'Second Corinthians 12', and begins reading in German. He finishes the passage, announces a prayer, flips the pages back to another bookmark at Matthew: 7, and reads the Lord's Prayer. He then closes the Bible, folds his hands, looks around at the expectant, waiting faces in the lamplight, and begins to explain the passage."

On the evening these notes were made, which turned out to be typical of many such services, he had read a passage concerning Paul and his conflict with Peter and the Disciples who knew Jesus. (Dr. Schweitzer discussed the meaning of this passage, which I have reported elsewhere.[7])

It was after such a service as this, on Monday, August 23, 1965, at the last supper taken with his staff that he gave instruction in the event of his death. A Swiss friend who reported that service told how he played the familiar hymns on the old piano, then read the Lord's Prayer in both German and French. Instead of a dissertation, he cleared his throat and told how he wanted the staff to carry on at his death.

The Republic of Gabon became an independent member of the French community in 1958, following a plebiscite. Hospital physicians and nurses have related how Africans came in daily with little slips of paper—ballots—and lined up at the Pharmacy and Dispensary to ask the attendants: "What does this mean?" Patiently, the staff would explain that they were now being given an opportunity to choose between becoming an independent nation or remaining a French dependency, as they were. Each had been given two slips of paper

[7] See *Faith and Freedom,* Vol. 16, No. 48, Part 3, Summer 1963, Manchester College (Oxford), England, and *The Unitarian Christian,* Vol. 18, No. 4, July 1963 (347 Marlborough St. Boston, Mass.).

headed Referendum. One was blue and marked *"Non"* and one was yellow and marked "Oui." They were simply to make the decision by turning in the proper slip. Often puzzled, the natives would ask, "But how can we vote for Dr. Schweitzer?"[8]

The coming of independence brought a whole new group of concerns and problems to the hospital, although life went on substantially as before. Dr. Schweitzer was and remained non-political in the African situation. However, emerging, independent Africa is extremely political and conscious of the political ramifications of all details and facets of its culture and society. This is not to say that all Africans were; however, the politically oriented persons who are vying for power and leadership in these fresh, lucrative lands where the old order has vanished were very alert to the nuances of politics and nationalism.

There exist two Africas, side by side and intertwined: the Africa of the native villages and common people whom Schweitzer used to call "the children of nature," and the Africa of the native intellectual. Years ago, Dr. Schweitzer used to relate the story of how, when building the hospital, he was straining to move a log while a well-dressed native in European clothing watched. The Doctor called out to the African to lend a hand. The African haughtily replied, "What? Me? I am an intellectual and don't do menial labor."

"You're lucky," Dr. Schweitzer replied. "I too wanted to become an intellectual but I didn't succeed."[9]

A former head of one of the Afro-American committees, operating in the United States to increase understanding and cooperation on the part of Americans with the problems of the emergent African nations, said in an address: "Even an Albert Schweitzer, and I honor and revere his example of personal renunciation for human service . . . could go to Africa and spend a lifetime with the Africans—and a lifetime of unremitting study, research, thought, and writing . . . about what?—about Western Christianity, without discovering that

[8] See Christensen, *Op. cit.*, for one account, pp. 36-37.
[9] See *On the Edge of the Primeval Forest*, p. 182.

the religion and the culture of Africa might be worthy of note . . . ."

This person, who respected Dr. Schweitzer and was obviously acquainted with those aspects of his writings that interest European and American scholarship, was apparently ignorant of the very minute attention which Dr. Schweitzer gave to African culture and development. The several preceding chapters have indicated his very great interest and appreciation of African culture. In addition, he was one of the few people who pointed out the dangers of breaking down the religious ideas and practices of the African; in fact he was considered in many quarters *persona non grata* because of his failure to support the African missionary conversion effort as a good in itself. His very hospital has been under attack because he created an institution which melded with the cultural traditions, rather than one which forced change in the African way of life at the moment when the patients would be powerless to resist—during suffering.

Dr. Schweitzer, in regard to Africa as in so much else, was an individualist and a non-conformist. He held his own position—not that which was popular. He followed no "line" and joined no popular majority. He did not, therefore, take a position which endeared him to those who say: "One hundred per cent Africa for the Africans," and on the other hand he did not support the position which says: "The Africans will be sorry they drove out and took over from the Europeans." Dr. Schweitzer saw what happened in Africa during World War I when most Europeans withdrew and the colonial administration was diverted to war matters, so that the colonial veneer was stripped away. Accordingly, he saw too much to close his eyes and say, "Africa can now exist without European-American assistance and contact." In fact, the situation during the first years of the Belgian withdrawal in the Congo verified his position: a precipitous withdrawal is damaging alike to Africans and to whites. A more gradual process is essential.

In my talks with Dr. Schweitzer, his concern for the African situation emerged. He said, for instance, when we were speaking about the danger of World War III, that "there is no problem of the Africans which they cannot solve themselves if the civilized nations of Europe and America do not blow themselves and Africa up first."

In 1927, Dr. Schweitzer wrote an article, published in the January 28 issue of the *Contemporary Review,* entitled *Relations of the White and Colored Races.* This article is still referred to, in part, because in it Dr. Schweitzer seemingly took for granted the continuation of colonialism in Africa. Who, one might ask, did not at that time. Africa has moved unbelievably fast since that time.

Dr. Schweitzer's basic approach is that the African system, in its own right and without need for apology, is valuable. This was part of his break with the missionaries. He was content to "save the bodies and not souls." He was content to accept them for themselves, with their own ideas, culture and standards of living; he did not try to force the white man's concepts on them.

In Africa, the charge of colonialism is a serious one, and all vestiges of it are held suspect. To many hotheaded young Africans all white people are under suspicion. Dr. Schweitzer was accused of being a white man and of having been there under colonial administrations, which fact made him suspect. All white people who remain in Africa today do so only under the terms of being political non-entities. They must be silent and leave African destiny to the native Africans. They cannot stay if they are not neutral. The Africans who charge that Dr. Schweitzer did not speak out for African independence would most likely be the first to shout "interference!" if he did.

It is possibly true that Dr. Schweitzer's ideas did not move as fast as those of many Africans. Perhaps there was a hesitancy as to which course was the wisest. There may have been an area of just plain not knowing. He may have been politically astute enough to sense that it was more likely to be reckless to speak out than to remain silent. However, was it necessary for Dr. Schweitzer to speak out to show his respect and interest in the African as a person? He spent fifty years in the privation of a jungle medical settlement to aid and assist Africans—not the sophisticated and cultured metropolitan Africans of the great capital cities of Africa, but those who live in the bush. Most of the self-styled liberals and modern African enthusiasts have not earned their right to be taken as seriously as Dr. Schweitzer. An allegedly critical writer like McKnight never bothered to try and get close to an African to find out his opinion of Schweitzer, or if he did, did not bother to quote. This is probably too often true: the doctrinaire liberal who attacked or challenged Schweitzer often did not bother to consider the African as a person.

The independence of Gabon evolved following the first general elections held at that time. Although Dr. Schweitzer tried to be non-political in this situation, it was difficult because the opposition parties, struggling for power, clutched every possible straw to embarrass the incumbent administration. For instance, during the 1960 "Independence Election," first general election for government officials, all contending political parties finally got together and joined a coalition, supporting M. Leon MBa, the outstanding Gabonese intellectual, for President. Many in the area of Lambaréné wrote in "ASB"—the designation used on all Schweitzer hospital equipment. During the campaign, at political rallies, after M. MBa and other coalition leaders had presented their cases, natives would then stand and ask: "Can we vote for M. Le Grand Docteur Schweitzer?" At no point did anyone on the hospital staff encourage such sentiments; indeed, every effort was made to discourage them. But many of the Africans in the tribes and villages who had turned to Dr. Schweitzer over the years viewed the changes ominously. They needed to be assured that the new ways would not deny them the continued services or the guidance of Le Grand Docteur and his hospital. However, their concern was sometimes interpreted as an unseemly dependence on a white man.

During the elections these genuine grass root expressions of reliance upon Dr. Schweitzer appeared as a threat to the new government and to the intellectual elite who were battling for power to replace the departing French leadership.

"Africa for the Africans" was a natural slogan. Two young political aspirants one day marched into the Schweitzer hospital and summoned all Africans to an assembly, announcing that "Dr. Schweitzer and his hospital are trespassers in Africa. Their concession is from the Colonial Government which is now deposed. Dr. Schweitzer should go home." The natives responded: "Non, Non, Non." Failing to arouse a demonstration, the political workers departed by boat as they had come. On the island of Lambaréné, the third largest community of the Republic, African political leaders proclaimed: "The missions, the hospital, and the lumber company must have new leadership. The Europeans must go home and leave our country to us." But the fact is that without the missions at Lambaréné—Catholic and Protestant—there would be no education; without the lumber company, the economy would not function; without the white medical staff, there would be no hospitals. There is no doubt, of course, that soon the Africans will be able to run their entire economy, education, and health services. Much of the protest is not to be taken any more seriously than statements made during American political campaigns. We were brought up short one day on a jungle road when a young man carrying a transistor radio asked: "Today at four o'clock, President Kennedy's Medicare program was defeated in the United States Senate;does this mean President Kennedy has been discredited?" We were so far away from Washington, and out of touch, that we did not even know the Medicare program was up for vote, but we tried to explain that American politicians took such things in stride. So do African politicians. Single votes, speeches or demonstrations are parts, not the total picture. We must remember that the African opposition that attacks such whites as Schweitzer is a small minority.

More significant is the very real popularity of the Schweitzer hospital, thronged daily by hundreds of Africans. All the time we were in Lambaréné, six or seven hundred Africans a day kept coming and going freely at the hospital. The Schweitzer hospital was jokingly referred to as "the fourth largest city in the Republic of Gabon." In contrast are the new Government hospitals, often with more empty beds than occupied ones; too, they must also rely on European doctors.

After returning to the United States I heard of new demonstrations at Lambaréné and wrote to the United States Ambassador to Gabon, the Hon. Charles F. Darlington, who answered me on March 19, 1963:

> I am pleased to reply to your letter of March 14, concerning your interest in Dr. Schweitzer and his hospital. Let me assure you at once that neither is in any way "in jeopardy." The hospital continues its work as always, and Gabonese from the surrounding area continue to flock to it. There are, of course, varying attitudes among Gabonese concerning Le Grand Docteur: many respect and admire him; some only tolerate him. The Government of Gabon gives the works its support. What course the hospital will take when Dr. Schweitzer passes from the scene is of course impossible to say; its future will probably be determined in part by those at the hospital and connected with the Schweitzer Foundations, and in part by the Gabonese Government.

When we were in Libreville, Ambassador Darlington was at the Schweitzer hospital, so we were not able to talk with him at the American Embassy. He had just left the hospital when we arrived there. We learned, however, that he had first-hand knowledge of the hospital, and we can therefore adjudge his assessment as reliable and fair.

Chapter 8

WHY WAS SCHWEITZER UNDER ATTACK?

"Jungle Doctor, Go Home" was reportedly chanted at the Schweitzer hospital during the political elections of 1963 by the opposition party. This is a variant on the familiar chants: "White Man, Go Home"; "Lumber Man, Go Home"; "Missionary, Go Home"; and "Boss Man, Go Home." All represent the seething unrest of new countries in Africa that have seen the power shifted from European administrators to the native populations. In Dr. Schweitzer's case, there were two political overtones to the opposition party's use of him as a symbol. The established Government of Gabon, headed by the Coalition Party of M. Leon MBa, had honored Dr. Schweitzer—a white man—in significant ways. It put out a beautiful airmail stamp with his picture on it. In addition, M. MBa, President of the Republic, visited the hospital and awarded him the *Etoile du Gabon,* the highest honor of Gabon. Consequently, opposition candidates thought they could embarrass the government if they could embarrass Dr. Schweitzer. Dr. Schweitzer took absolutely no political position on the internal affairs of Gabon. He neither defended nor answered such charges. He let his work at the hospital stand on its own merits.

Like many other white men who had lived the better part of their lives in Africa, he looked upon Africa as his home. Many African countries are now asking all residents to renounce citizenship in other countries if they wish to remain in Africa. What Dr. Schweitzer's answer would be is conjecture, but he said to me, "I am an old man who has lived most of my life in Africa, and here I will remain." He declined to return to Europe or America because, "My Africans will not understand if I should leave them at the end."

There is a revealing account that has made the rounds of certain European journals touching upon the explosive situation of African relationships—an account that we should briefly summarize here. The most accessible English language version is to be found in *The News Digest of the I.A.R.F.*, No. 50, February 1963, which is published in The Hague, The Netherlands, at 40 Laan Copes van Cattenburch. This issue refers to the *Der Spiegel* criticisms of Dr. Schweitzer. The defense and analysis of that attack appeared in the Paris journal *Evangile et Liberté* for November 1962. The Paris rebuttal pointed out that the *Der Spiegel* article drew heavily from *Jeune Afrique, (Young Africa)* which publishes strident, anti-white articles, often of an inflammatory nature. It used Schweitzer as an example of white men in Africa who had been supported by colonial administrations and charged that his hospital was beneath the dignity of the "new African."

Both the Paris and Hague journals pointed out that the temper of the journalism in *Jeune Afrique* is such that all one needed to be was a European in order to face accusations. Accordingly, they suggested that *Der Spiegel* should have examined the motivations before spreading the anti-Schweitzer attack throughout Europe. These attacks were used by Gerald McKnight as authoritative evidence in his volume referred to in earlier chapters of this book.

Some of the African criticism is undoubtedly based on no more reason than the fact that Dr. Schweitzer was a white man in a land of emerging black men seeking to prove their own equality with the former colonial administrators.

In the autumn of 1962 there was a widely quoted press release from Southern Rhodesia commenting on African criticism of Dr. Schweitzer. This article summed up reasons for the criticism. It read in part: "A statement attributed to him that 'Africa would be beautiful without its savages' is calculated to bespeak indignation from every African nationalist who hears it." The sad fact is that this statement is taken out of context. What Dr. Schweitzer was really saying, if the entire passage is read, was that Africa would be beautiful if it were not for the sickness and suffering of the Africans, which casts a cloud over the otherwise tranquil beauty of Africa. It is the doctor in him that was speaking, not a colonialist. It was his compassion for these people who "know the terrible lord whose name is Pain." He wrote: "Physical misery is great everywhere out here. Are we justified in shutting our eyes? . . ." However, this news article, asserting African sensitivity to Schweitzer, said that he represented both a "White superiority" and "the establishment" which is in the process of being overthrown. Inasmuch as such attacks were and still are being made, those who know better need to speak out.

It is undeniable that such criticism is heard. An experience comes to mind. One of the strange facts that impresses the traveler in Africa today is the lack of knowledge of Africans concerning Dr. Schweitzer's work and his attitudes. We once sat in the home of a highly respected government official—a member of the National Parliament—in Eastern Nigeria. "What do you think of Dr. Schweitzer?" I asked him.

The well-trained and articulate leader, representative of the new African statesman, educator and administrator, replied: "These missionaries have been too much concerned with the saving of souls, even when they were practicing medicine or teaching agriculture. Our tempo is too fast. We do not have time for them. We must move at a faster rate than the missionary, and so he does not understand us, nor we him."

Trying to explain, I said, "You have missed the point about Dr. Schweitzer. He is a doctor more than a missionary. Many church people in America are upset that he ministers only to the bodies and not to the souls. This is the main criticism of him in our country. Have you ever seen him, or talked with him?" I asked.

"No, not him. But what I have said is the attitude of the New Africa."

Later, in Lagos, I met with a talkative Nigerian. Unlike the Member of Parliament, he had never been out of his country.

"Do you know anything about Dr. Schweitzer?" I asked.

"Oh, yes, I know about him. Most of us in Lagos moved here from other places. We came in from the bush and in our villages we knew teachers and doctors who were missionaries. They would come to our village and they would say, 'We are a doctor; we are a teacher; we are a farmer; and we are going to show you how to do things. We are like Dr. Schweitzer. We are coming to help you.' And so they set up their missions and they worked with our people. If our people liked the missionary, then they liked Dr. Schweitzer because he was like Dr. Schweitzer. But, if our people did not like the missionary, then they didn't like Dr. Schweitzer. Sometimes they didn't like the missionary. He wanted them to give him too many presents. He wanted them to become a Christian in return for which he would kill their sickness, or educate their children, or show them how to raise better chickens or to grow better food. It was necessary to accept his God and to renounce the old gods and many of our people did not like the missionaries who asked them to do this. Then they would think they did not like Dr. Schweitzer either."

The sad fact is, of course, that missionaries are looked upon as part of the old order of colonial rule which is passé. Africans love to tell you that their new states guarantee complete equality of religion for all religions: Christian, Moslem and African. Many Christian practices taught by the missionaries are being critically re-examined and quickly abandoned. The emerging African culture demands a flexibility that is often seemingly hampered by the strictures of the missionary, whose morality, customs, religious teachings and Bible are often looked upon as unwanted imports. The missionary is associated with the teachings of colonialism; for decades he seemingly supported the position that every man has a place and belongs in it. This was too often interpreted to mean the African was subservient to the white man. Christianity is, accordingly, looked upon as "the white man's religion." This is not so with Islam or the animistic African religions, those tribal beliefs invoking "The Great Gods of Africa." Christianity insisted upon monogamous marriage—only one wife at a time—which is often contrary to tribal patterns.

An editorial in a Lagos paper while we were there pointed out that the Christian missionary teaching in this regard was "more primitive" and "less humane" than that of the African culture, for the African required that a man keep and provide for an unwanted wife rather than turn her out. Islam agrees with the African tribal patterns in its concept of polygamy, and seems more adaptable to Africa.

Christianity in Africa—the missionary represents Christianity there—has been under attack for its methods of procedure, which tended to give the appearance of collaboration with the colonial administrations; also because it attacked and undermined existing cultural patterns. Those who knew nothing about Dr. Schweitzer, except that he was *called* a missionary, therefore condemned him along with all missionaries.

Most Africans know nothing of those in other parts of Africa. As already noted, the river valley circumscribes the entire knowledge of Africa for most. Those in the Niger River Valley know little of the Ogowe Valley or the Congo Valley. Accordingly, knowledge of Dr. Schweitzer outside of the Ogowe River Valley is filled with error.

The independent African of today is a fiercely proud representative of a new way of life emerging on the world stage. It grieves him that the one person practically every white man who comes to Africa inquires about is not an African leader but a white doctor. If the first person asked about was Nkrumah, Mboya, Kenyatta or Dr. Azikiwe, they would be much happier. But, no, the white man usually starts a conversation by saying, "What do you think about Dr. Schweitzer?"

In addition to the African attack on Dr. Schweitzer as a missionary, the missionaries themselves, and the Christian churches in Europe and America, often joined in the accusations against him and took a secret pleasure in the attacks on the part of the Africans.

The major reason for the attacks on Dr. Schweitzer in our day may well be attributed to certain religious issues which have rallied persons against him. What are these religious issues that are so disquieting?

One was the fear that there was a growing tendency in his thought toward a secularized point of view. He moved from being primarily a preacher to being primarily a physician, and in later years he characterized himself as a scientist.

He moved out of the mission to establish an independent hospital. Many persons even today are shocked to learn that he was not really a missionary.

Then there was the fear of the growing liberalism of Dr. Schweitzer. It was in fact not growing; only becoming better known. When he identified himself as a Unitarian in 1961 many of his friends at the Schweitzer hospital said: "If people would have read his books, they would have understood this, but many of them love and believe in him because of the example he has given them through his practice of the ethics of religion, and so they are stunned."

Actually, Dr. Schweitzer was one of the few great churchmen who, during the bitter period after World War I and throughout World War II, remained a committed liberal in religion. He stood almost alone in this position, with a few notable exceptions such as Dr. Rufus Jones, Dr. Harry Emerson Fosdick and the Dean of Canterbury. Of course, the small sects of Unitarians, Universalists and Quakers continued throughout this period to cherish the values of religious liberalism; however, the great bulk of Protestant churches reverted to orthodoxy. One of the important interpreters of Dr. Schweitzer, George Seaver, wrote of an historic meeting between Schweitzer and the great neo-orthodox minister, Dr. Karl Barth, in Munster, Switzerland. Schweitzer said to Barth, "You and I started from the same problem, the disintegration of modern thought, but whereas you went back to the Reformation, I went back to the Enlightenment."[1]

It was in this light that Eugene Exman, in his perceptive essay on Dr. Schweitzer in the photographic volume by Erica Anderson, wrote: "In the field of theology the names of Schweitzer and Karl Barth are likely to be joined for a very different reason. The theological controversy currently en-

1 George Seaver, *Albert Schweitzer: Christian Revolutionary,* New York, Harper, 1944, pp. 42-43.

gaging Protestantism finds Schweitzer at the opposite pole from his Swiss contemporary."[2]

When the Doctor told Norman Cousins[3] of his religious evolution from orthodoxy, he added: "What was I to do? . . . I determined I would make my life my argument." For half a century his life was indeed the argument for the things he believed—the practice of liberal religion and of the ethics of Jesus as he understood it. He never asked for favor or consideration. He said that when he was ordained by the Lutheran Synod of Strasbourg, he knew then that there was not another synod of the Lutheran Church that would have ordained him, because of the heresies he had already put into print. "But they stood by me through the years, and it would be undignified and unmanly for me to desert them now." Consequently, he did not withdraw from the Lutherans, and he said, "They do not understand that the Unitarians have not asked that I do so."

Time magazine once asked him about his dual religious loyalty, and reported:[4] "His own eclectic exegesis: 'For a long time now I have had connections with the Unitarian Church. Yet there is no question of breaking with the Lutheran Church. I am a Protestant, but above all I am a scientist and as such I can be on good terms with all Protestant churches.' As for the matter of the Trinity, which Lutherans affirm and Unitarians deny, Schweitzer wondered rhetorically, 'Did Christ or St. Paul believe it?' "

Dr. Gabriel Langfeldt has studied[5] the unorthodox religious views which have prompted many to ask: "Is Dr. Schweitzer a Christian or not?" He points out that Schweitzer has rejected such concepts as the traditional view of God, the assured efficacy of prayer, the supremacy of faith over reason, the deity of Christ, the sacraments, the virgin birth, atonement, resurrection, and the ascension. Carl Hermann Voss,

[2] Erica Anderson and Eugene Exman, *The World of Albert Schweitzer*, New York, Harper, 1955, p. 109.

[3] Cousins, *op. cit.*, p. 191.

[4] *Time* Magazine, December 8, 1961.

[5] Gabriel Langfeldt, *Op. cit.*

who reviewed the book for the *Saturday Review,*[6] summarized the conclusions (as well as the categories quoted above) by saying that Dr. Langfeldt's answer to whether Schweitzer was a Christian or not was: "What difference does it make when one considers the practical application of Christian virtues and ethics?"

The American attack on Schweitzer may be viewed through the pages of the popular and widely circulated fortnightly journal *Christianity Today,* which in an article entitled *Sacrifice Without End*[7] by Editorial Associate James Daane, commented on an anthology of Schweitzer's writings (*Pilgrimage to Humanity*). Mr. Daane, in the course of his article, wrote, "Deep and sensitive spirit that he is, Schweitzer all his life wrestled with the awful fact of suffering. But he found no solution. He insists that life even in its lowest form must be reverenced. . . . 'I cannot avoid reflecting that, in order to preserve life, I have to destroy other life' (Schweitzer, p. 89). Here he (Schweitzer) is nigh unto the Kingdom but remains outside. He ends with a universe in which what is allegedly the highest and most sacred, namely life, is sacrificed for its own sake. For Schweitzer who insists on a rational universe, this is a cosmic element of jolting irrationality. While in Christianity the highest, the Son of God, is sacrificed for sinners, and thus with rational purpose. Schweitzer has not gotten beyond a highest which is sacrificed for itself, and thus to no rational purpose. . . . Schweitzer is a man of uncommon dimension. Yet the story of his life and thought as a 'road to humanity' will in reading appear to the Christian as a kind of *via dolorosa.* Schweitzer has sacrificed without Christ, and therefore has made a pilgrimage without end."

Since the journal in which these words appeared is one of the most highly regarded as well as most widely circulated organs of American Protestant evangelical faith, these sentiments—expressed by a member of the editorial staff—may be viewed as representative of the intellectual negation of Dr. Schweitzer's liberal Christianity by orthodoxy.

6 *Saturday Review,* January 14, 1961.
7 *Christianity Today,* February 16, 1962, pp. 43-44.

In 1947, the International Association for Liberal Christianity and Religious Freedom, whose headquarters are in The Hague, invited Dr. Schweitzer to address its international triennial congress in Bern, Switzerland. Unable to leave Lambaréné in time, but mindful of the importance of this congress for the worldwide community of Unitarian and other liberal religious affiliates composing its national component groups, Dr. Schweitzer sent a message to be read, which said in part:

> In this Conference, do not hide from the fact that you serve an unpopular cause! Liberal Christianity is as unpopular today as it ever has been, because the dominant spirit of our time attempts to smother liberal religious thinking. On the other hand, it is a timely cause—as timely as ever—because it is a necessity for the spiritual life of our age. Only through a renewal of ethical and religious thought can the spirit arise which imparts to mankind the knowledge and power necessary for the pilgrimage from darkness and strife to light and peace. Liberal Christianity has the magnificent responsibility of communicating and upholding the conviction that thought and religion are not incompatible but belong together. Every deep piety is reflective; every really deep thought is reverent.

He then continued:

> As we speak for liberal Christianity and expect men to arrive at religious positions by their own thinking, we have before us the image of Jesus, who insisted that one should not, in the name of religion, place on men's shoulders improper and heavy burdens. . . . May your liberal Christianity prove effective in spirit and deed in accomplishing its tasks in our day. . . . Our ideal is not merely liberal Christianity but the most profound Christianity.[8]

Dr. Schweitzer earlier wrote, "The satisfaction that I could not help feeling at having solved so many historical riddles about the existence of Jesus was accompanied by the painful

[8] Essay on "Liberal Christianity" in Albert Schweitzer, *Pilgrimage to Humanity*, New York, Philosophical Library, 1961, pp. 74-75.

consciousness that this new knowledge in the realm of history would mean unrest and difficulty for Christian piety."[9] Accordingly, Dr. Schweitzer, who was true to the principle of historical objectivity and truth, was unhappy over upsetting Christian faith; not only orthodox Christianity, but liberal Christianity. He goes on to point this out: "I myself have suffered in this matter by having had to join in the work of destroying the portrait of Christ on which liberal Christianity based its appeal. At the same time I was convinced that this liberal Christianity was not reduced to living on an historical illusion, but could equally appeal to the Jesus of history, and further, that it carried its justification in itself."[10]

But it was not the liberal Christian who attacked Schweitzer. He tended to accept Schweitzer's verdict that the Jesus of history does not rest on an historical illusion, and that truthfulness and objectivity carry their own justification. However, this affirmative vision of Dr. Schweitzer helped to show the gulf existing between his religious thought and that of the orthodoxy which felt itself challenged by the great Doctor of the African jungle. For years it dared not really strike back at Dr. Schweitzer on theological, historical or philosophical grounds. Later, however, when it saw Dr. Schweitzer being attacked for other reasons, it joined in the efforts to discredit him, knowing that, human nature being what it is, the discrediting of Schweitzer in one area would cast doubt over all areas of his endeavor.

There was another group of people who attacked Dr. Schweitzer, those who could not "sell" him on a program. He did not lend himself to manipulation by any person or group. His hospital was not for sale to journalistic hucksters any more than it was for publicity gimmicks or slick fund raising schemes. He seemed immovable and uncorruptible. Many came to him with offers to raise the badly needed funds to extend and expand the facilities of the struggling jungle hospital. Patiently, Dr. Schweitzer would listen to the proposals, and then would ask, "What must I do?" Then would

[9] *Out of My Life and Thought,* p. 65.
[10] *Ibid.,* p. 73.

come the procedures of successful promotion. He would have to allow his name to be signed to letters and statements, carefully worded by "experts." He would have to make some personal appearances. Write-up men, ad men, photographers, television cameramen and recorders, etc., would come to the hospital for the preparation of audio-visual materials. "No!" he would say, shaking his massive head. "It is out of character." He knew above all else he could not be fitted into the mold of either the successful salesman or the organization man.

His sense of humility was humbling to all, until someone would become superficial and glib. They then learned instantly that the Doctor was no fool. He was an intellectual, and more than that he was exceedingly tough-minded and hard-headed, in the best and most exacting sense of these words. Dr. Schweitzer allowed no foggy notions to float through a discussion without pouncing upon them. He would not sit quietly by and permit statements made which the spokesman was not prepared to back up, defend and explain. No superficial exegesis of a problem, and no shallow conclusions were allowed to go without clarification. Anyone who established a good relationship with Dr. Schweitzer had to be intellectually honest. It was not necessary that he be able to converse on the level of an Einstein, but he could not try to give the impression that he could do so when he couldn't. Dr. Schweitzer, as a warm human, accepted anybody on his own level, so long as he did not "put on airs" of intellectual superiority. I suspect that most of the unfavorable reports brought back from Africa concerning Schweitzer came from those who "were put in their place" for too glib or superficial statements which he challenged. Only thus can I account for the charges of "authoritarian," "autocratic," or "old-fashioned," which from time to time made their way into print. The warmness, love, devotion and confidence so many held for "le grand Docteur" belied such spurious charges. He was no more authoritarian than any hospital administrator or executive director who must administer and direct. It is true that hospital policy was not set by vote of the patients, but then, where is it?

The trials and tribulations which Doctor Schweitzer went through with reporters and professional exposé artists created vexing experiences for members of the hospital staff. Mrs. Lotte Gerhold, an Austrian secretary and old time friend of Dr. Schweitzer, who regularly spent half of every year at the hospital helping the Doctor with his correspondence and visitors, recently wrote this account, after I had inquired concerning the report in a magazine referred to earlier in this chapter. She wrote in part:

> Often, since I had your letter, I tried to figure out in my mind who was this reporter. There are so many journalists who come here, and stay such a short time, that one doesn't really notice them. I remember fairly well a rather shy journalist who felt sick while he was here, and who stayed in the hotel in Lambaréné. I believe he was from Rhodesia. There was an English reporter who was a decent chap. Then I remember another one with very disrespectful manners. This young fellow came into the Pharmacy, seating himself at once on the table behind Dr. Schweitzer's back, and started to smoke, blowing great clouds of smoke over Dr. Schweitzer's head, until Dr. Schweitzer asked him to please not smoke in the Pharmacy. He had a very disrespectful way of addressing Dr. Schweitzer. As he came from Algiers, Dr. Schweitzer asked him what he thought about the situation there. He replied tartly that he did not think it his task to form any opinion. That's all I remember about this journalist. As I recall, he never mentioned his name or what paper he wrote for. I asked Miss Ali Silver, the senior staff member, and she did not know either. Of course, Dr. Schweitzer is not at work on Volume III of his Philosophy of Civilization, and has not for many years. We see these scandalous "reports" about the hospital by "writers" who do not really try to get a picture of the hospital.

This description by a person close to Dr. Schweitzer at the hospital shows how superficial is the analysis of the hospital by many reporters. I had asked her originally about an account which said the Doctor was working on Volume III, because Schweitzer specifically had told me he was not and that "there is no longer a need to complete my *Philosophy of Civilization.*" Accordingly, when I read the article I was immediately suspicious that such writers had not really become compatible with Dr. Schweitzer at all. Mrs. Gerhold's letter would seem to confirm it.

Thus we see that there are many reasons why the Doctor was attacked by different people. To what extent were they justified? We have implied a partial answer, but let us look at the most crucial area—the hospital itself.

Chapter 9

WAS THE GOOD DOCTOR GOOD ENOUGH?

One seldom discussed Dr. Schweitzer in his final years without reservations being expressed. These may have taken any number of directions. One person, now in the performing arts in New York City, was heard recently to groan, "Not Saint Schweitzer again!" when his name was mentioned. A young doctor in Boston recently gained a hearing at a cocktail party by proclaiming that "Dr. Schweitzer has set the practice of medicine in Africa back fifty years!"

A recent correspondent (an American working in Paris) who had read not only my articles but those of another visitor to Lambaréné, wrote: "Against what you both state, medical people are very little impressed with the old-time doctoring of the Lambaréné hospital; people feel there is no attention at all paid to modern science in the hospital's daily routine. Would you care to comment? . . . I am a great admirer of much I have read of Schweitzer, but agree his record of colonialism is also questionable from what others say."

In Africa, I once sat next to a Dutch lumberman who doubled as Consul for the Netherlands. He exclaimed that the Schweitzer hospital was primitive. Upon questioning him, I learned he had been there twice, and that the total amount of time he spent there was less than a half hour. His main complaint was that the goat droppings made it necessary to be careful where one stepped on the paths. I thought of the curbed dogs on Manhattan as well as Amsterdam sidewalks.

It is on grounds such as these that many of the criticisms

are made. That Dr. Schweitzer is glorified by some makes others all the more demanding in their expectations of him. Dr. Schweitzer would have been the last to call himself a saint. He asserted to us that "I am only a person trying to live my religion."

Dr. Dana McLean Greeley, President of the Unitarian Universalist Association, responded by saying, "You have done superbly," whereupon the Doctor objected emphatically.

"No!" he exclaimed, swinging his hands through the air as though to expunge the words. "That is not yours to say! Only when I climb the pearly stairs and my book is closed can the answer be given." Then, changing his tone and with the twinkle returning to his eyes, he chuckled. "But it will be just my luck to be met by St. Peter. And do you know what he will say? 'But first, tell me to which church do you belong?' " The private joke about church membership between the head of the Unitarian Universalists and the Doctor of Lambaréné was not without its point. However, for us, the fact that he would brook no superlatives, even from a head of a church, is sufficient proof that Dr. Schweitzer harbored no illusions of saintliness. Most mortals will venerate a dead saint, but find a living one tedious and hard to take. To the extent that he had been called a saint, Schweitzer has been held more rigorously accountable than any other.

My correspondent from Paris is guilty in reverse for his over-strong statement. Just as the exaggerated claims of saintliness may be too extreme for any mortal man, so are the references to "old-time doctoring" and "no attention paid to modern science." Modern medical methods, up-to-date therapy, drugs, procedures and knowledge have been the stock in trade of the Schweitzer hospital. My friend oversimplified and reduced to exaggerated absurdity the current criticism. But what is the real basis for medical criticism?

Norman Cousins, in his book, related that before he left New York, Clara Urquhart, who was to travel with him as his photographer-collaborator and who knew Dr. Schweitzer from earlier visits, tried to prepare him for what he would see:

"Now," she said, "comes the most important matter of all. You've got to promise that you won't be disillusioned."

I smiled. "You mean a hospital ward without bedsheets, lack of sanitation, and all that sort of thing?" I said. "Please don't let it worry you; I know all about it. It was this kind of argument that seemed to me all along to miss the main point about Schweitzer."

"There's something more important than that," she replied. "I'm talking about Schweitzer himself."

This startled me. "Why is there any danger that I or anyone else would be disillusioned about Schweitzer?"

"Some people are. They come to Lambaréné with an image of a sort of sweet saintly Saint Francis feeding the birds and they see instead a driving man fighting the jungle and African lethargy and they do not remain for a sufficiently long period to see or sense the goodness and saintliness underneath. They go away feeling hurt and unhappy."

I was touched by her concern but still puzzled. What was there about Schweitzer that created "hurt and unhappy" feelings in people? Whatever the answer, I couldn't guarantee Clara Urquhart what my feelings would be after I met him.

"Of course not," she said. "I just want to be sure you'll stay long enough to get over the first impressions that may not be so favorable."

"Such as?"

"Such as the fact that those who do not know the Doctor will think that his manner toward the indigene or black is unfeeling and authoritarian. Such as the fact that his views seem to reflect little confidence in the Africans to whom he has given his life. Schweitzer has deeper and wider dimensions than anyone else I have met. If I evaluated from a superficial viewpoint the image is distorted. For better or for worse Schweitzer is a patriarch. I remember saying to him that he was an enlightened despot—to which he replied: 'An enlightened despot is able to give the greatest amount of freedom.' If one fails to remember that his basic motivation is' reverence for life—he might seem arbitrary in his dealings with those around him. Just wait and observe for the first few days." [1]

[1] Cousins, *op. cit.,* pp. 19-20.

After visiting the hospital, Norman Cousins evaluated it this way:

> Walking around the Hospital with George Malthen as my guide, I could understand why some visitors came away with negative impressions.
>
> The idea of a hospital creates instant images in the mind of immaculate corridors, white sheets, total sanitation. These images were badly jolted when one saw the Hospital at Lambaréné for the first time. Countless numbers of goats wandered at will all over the place; even when they were not visible their presence was perceptible. The ground was made moist and slippery by an equally large number of chickens. Hanging heavily in the dank air was the smoke from the dozens of crude burners used by the Africans for their cooking. There was also an inexplicably sweet and somewhat sticky smell—perhaps from the cooking or from fallen and fermented fruit. The sanitary facilities were at an absolute minimum. There were only two outhouses, one for each sex. The sewer underneath was open and sometimes the wind blew from the wrong direction.
>
> There were no bedsheets. The Africans brought their own blankets. There were no "wards" as the term is used elsewhere. There were long bungalow-like affairs with small cubicles. When a patient came to the Hospital, he was generally accompanied by his entire family. The mother did the cooking, as she would at home. The children were usually on their own.
>
> The difficulty, of course, was with the term "hospital" as applied to the Schweitzer colony. It created false images and expectations by outsiders. The proper term should be "jungle clinic," as Dr. Margaret had explained. Dr. Schweitzer did not come to Africa for the purpose of building a towering medical center. He came in order to meet the Africans on their own terms. What he built was an African village attached to a functional medical and surgical clinic. The Africans were attracted to Schweitzer because of the man himself and because this was a village and a way of life familiar to them rather than a forbidding building where they would be cut off from their families and frightened by a world of total whiteness, of people and walls

and machines. Modern medicine has come to accept the emotional security of the patient as a vital part of any therapy. Dr. Schweitzer knew this almost a half-century earlier when he made his plans to serve in Africa. Most visitors who stayed long enough became aware of these things. While they might never be able to accept completely all the crudeness, at least they developed a working perspective. Some visitors, however, could hardly wait to get back to Europe or America in order to make their own discoveries. I had read at least four articles by disillusioned visitors to Lambarene who misunderstood and misjudged Dr. Schweitzer and what he was trying to do in Africa.[2]

The odd aspect of much of the criticism of this type of African hospital is that it comes from the "wrong people," that is, from people who otherwise condemn the indiscriminate ignoring and rough-shod trampling of African ways in the rush to "modernize and civilize." Colonial insensitivity to the African is rightly condemned by many people. The neglect of African ways and the haughty superiority of many Europeans and Americans are properly to be criticized. Dr. Schweitzer, however, recognized and met the African culture on a creative level. The African was not made to feel inferior and primitive as he came into a strange, new, sterilized and sophisticated center which expected a wholly new set of responses from him. The African was "at home" and therefore "at ease" in the Schweitzer hospital. There was no need to overcome cultural and hence psychological handicaps before therapy could commence.

Naturally, there is a line between good medical practices, advanced methods and informed therapy on the one hand and superficial manifestations of a superior civilization on the other. The argument is almost one of whether you can have good medical care without having innerspring mattresses on white enamel bedsteads; of whether plumbing pipes and receptacles are the measure of sanitation; of whether or not picture windows and air conditioning can bring the comforts

[2] *Ibid.*, pp. 91-93.

of the white man to the jungle. How, for instance, would therapy progress when the native, acclimated to weeks of air conditioned living, returned to the bamboo hut with the leaf tile roof?

Would sewers clean up the jungle, or make more filthy the otherwise nearly perfect order of nature that is clean and purifying until defiled by the wastes of civilization? Even in the United States engineers are now discussing whether central sewers are in all cases desirable, even in cities, and whether cesspools and septic tanks may not be more sensible. Dr. Schweitzer suggested once that man has never improved on nature in sanitation methods: the tiny ants attacking the organic waste of life reconvert it to organic forms; life lives off of life, and lower forms of matter are reconstituted by and for higher forms.

Naturally, many Africans today seem to accept the idea that civilization and "arrival" demand the status symbol of sewers, pipes, and furniture. It can well be that they are mistaken.

When I was in Nigeria all the papers were discussing the urgent need for population growth in their country. "More babies" seemed to be a national propaganda slogan. Political leaders were saying that the rapidly expanding civilization of their country demanded a larger population. (At the same time the public officials of Lagos were concerned with the rising unemployment of the thousands of Nigerians from the bush who were deserting their tribal villages and settling in the city, where there was no likelihood of economic subsistence.) Recently, ominous reports of the dangers of the explosive growth of the Nigerian population show the folly of this policy. The weekly review *West Africa,* in its issue of February 29, 1964, reported in its lead story:

> From thirteenth in the world's population table, Nigeria has now moved up to ninth. According to the final census figure, Nigeria has now passed France, West Germany, Italy and the United Kingdom. Her population is 56 million . . . . gratifying though this evidence of Nigeria's importance must be to her leaders, the increased population over the

> figures of 1952-53 should deeply alarm them. For the increase is five and a half per cent a year. This is a rate without parallel in the world for a major country, and if continued, would confound all Nigeria's social and economic planning.[3]

The article continues by giving figures from the *U.N. Demographic Yearbook* which show that the rate of increase in the United States is 2.1 per cent; in Asia 1.8 per cent; and in Europe .7 per cent. In overpopulated Asia, the population density is 57 persons per square kilometer; in Africa as a whole, 7 persons; but in Nigeria it is 55. The population figures show that the Nigerian rate of growth means that in thirteen years her population will double—far exceeding that of Asia for population density. It is seriously doubted that she can grow food for 112 million people even though most Nigerian land may be populated (good bye to the jungle).

I quote this population development to show by statistics that an African point of view (such as the "More Babies" campaign) does not necessarily constitute what is best for Africans, just as an official American point of view does not necessarily reflect what is best for America. Just as some Africans say they are ready for modern hospitals, there may be others who need modern medicines but in the village compound setting of a Schweitzer hospital. Having visited several other African hospitals—walked down the still, quiet corridors, seen the silent, unhappy, vacant faces of the bedridden patients—I later thrilled to the sense of life and joy in the family atmosphere—somewhat boisterous and informal—at the Schweitzer hospital. Patients at the Schweitzer hospital were still living in their own world.

A zoologist from the Congo Republic (formerly the Belgian Congo) whose wife was a physiotherapist told me how, when the new million dollar hospital in Leopoldville was opened, the natives came in, placed their belongings on the beds, unrolled their straw mats and slept on the floor. The inspect-

[3] *West Africa,* No. 2439, Feb. 29, 1964, Overseas Newspapers (Agencies) Ltd., 9 New Fetter Lane, London E.C.4.

ing teams of government officials were irate and tried to force the natives to climb up on the beds. To a person who has never slept on a bed, this can be a frightening experience. Dr. Schweitzer, in contrast, conducted his hospital according to his view that when a person is suffering, one should not make him more insecure by changing his way of life and culture too. "It is hard enough to change our way of life when we are in good health," he said with a twinkle.

Dr. Schweitzer described himself as a slow moving rhinoceros from the African jungle who would not be stampeded. When one looks at recent pictures of Gabon's mechanized military units, of the female parachutists in their battle attire and weapons, one cannot wonder which type of civilization is really better for the African—that of the "civilization bringers," or that of the "shaggy old dog" near Lambaréné?

None of the reports critical of the hospital that have come to my attention are based on information of clinical failure or medical obsolescence, rather they are based on architecture —the type of structures: rough-hewn, mahogany, camp-style buildings—and on the question of preventive medicine and public health.

Dr. Paul Dudley White, the noted heart specialist, visited the Schweitzer hospital for the second time in the summer of 1963. "The hospital has a surprisingly good medical record," he said.[4] Noting that "Dr. Schweitzer and his staff were too busy meeting the needs of the sick to move into the field of preventive medicine," Dr. White added that "Just plain public health work such as clearing the swamps and ridding the region of mosquitoes" would cut Dr. Schweitzer's work in half.

Where, we must ask, can we find physicians who will go out and drain the swamps? Isn't this more a government's task, and the work of engineers rather than doctors? White himself would agree with this. Yet the crux of much criticism is that Dr. Schweitzer was too busy in the operating room to enter the public health field.

[4] *Boston Globe,* September 6, 1963: *Boston Sunday Herald,* September 8, 1963.

It goes without saying that any doctor who has been at the same practice for fifty years risks being called "old fashioned;" Dr. Schweitzer was no exception. However, Dr. Schweitzer built up a hospital that is independent of the need to rely on his medical skill alone.

The hospital uses modern techniques, medicines, and therapy. Dr. Schweitzer, with genuine delight, showed us the well-stocked Pharmacy saying, "It is your modern American drugs—the antibiotics—that cure so many of our old African diseases now." Among the diseases cured regularly are leprosy, malaria, gonorrhea, and sleeping sickness. The first day I was there a new electric microscope was being installed. Clinically and therapeutically, this hospital is an advanced institution, even though it is just a sprawling group of buildings in a jungle clearing and is overrun with small children and animals. It sometimes appears a bit hectic to visitors accustomed to the sterile, impersonal, antiseptic sanatoriums of our large cities.

Today there are many gleaming new hospitals in Africa, even in Gabon. The government has built large, new, "European-style" hospitals, including one on the island of Lambaréné, and probably some missions now have their own hospitals. However, the pattern of medicine in Africa, including Gabon, where doctors are scarce, is that major medical work and surgery is only done at the largest regional medical centers. By common consent, the Schweitzer hospital is so regarded. All surgical and major medical cases from the government hospital are transferred to the Schweitzer hospital, where the number of staff and the greater supply of medicines, drugs and skilled personnel insure adequate medical practices. Thus, even though there is a "gleaming new government hospital on the island of Lambaréné two miles away,"[5] it is not able to replace the Schweitzer hospital; it simply relieves it of minor medical cases so that the Schweitzer hospital can specialize more in acute medical cases and surgery. Perhaps, in time, the other hospitals will acquire the

[5] *Time* Magazine, June 21, 1963.

sufficient number of staff to branch out into surgery. When that day comes, their indebtedness to the Schweitzer hospital will be recognized.

We have already presented a picture of the Schweitzer hospital in the past several chapters. It would seem well now to summarize the scope of the hospital and its distinct features, which, admittedly different from European and American hospitals, may merely be unique applications of a hospital to the local conditions, rather than inferior conditions.

First of all, it should not be overlooked that the Schweitzer hospital does not really charge for its services. Dr. Schweitzer long ago decided that it was a good general policy to expect payment in some means, if the family could do so, more for psychological reasons than financial,[6] but service is never conditioned on ability to pay. If a family has a hen, a goat, some leaf tiles, produce, or whatever, it is considered to be negotiable goods and they may pay it. Labor also is a form of payment. However, no one is charged on a fee basis for room treatment or medicine, and there are none of the traditional "doctor's bills" or consultant's fees charged. There are no better rooms for those who can pay more. As previously stated, over nine tons of food is issued weekly by the hospital commissary to the patients' families. Hardly any of this is paid for. It was a service made available by Dr. Schweitzer through his own personal income; the royalties from his writings, the prizes (the Nobel Prize funds were used to build a Leper Village), the unsolicited grants from foundations and charitable organizations, and the numerous gifts from individuals. Dr. Schweitzer was most conscious of the latter group. When wine was served at one meal, he called aside the cook and manager of the dining room and said, "You know we are sent money by many widows and poor people; do you think they can drink wine with just an ordinary meal? We should not do anything here that they cannot do."

A second aspect beyond the charitable and free nature of the hospital's service to the African is the adaptable cultural

[6] *Out of My Life and Thought,* p. 167.

approach so easily misinterpreted by those who have not become attuned to the African village way of life. As we have indicated, Dr. Schweitzer believed that a sick person should not have his culture threatened at the very time he is insecure physically, emotionally and mentally. Much of the criticism of the hospital has come from people who failed to understand why the jungle natives were treated as natives rather than modern American bedridden patients. Dr. Schweitzer invited the sick to bring someone from his or her own family or tribe to care for and feed them; he thus overcame the superstitious fears rampant in the jungle. To have discovered such a simple way to assure peace of mind for the sick and fearful patient has been perhaps the most advanced therapy at the Schweitzer hospital, and the most misunderstood.

Finally, as already suggested, the Surgery of the Schweitzer hospital is an advanced center. It was as a surgeon that Dr. Schweitzer first gained the confidence of the African. His skill with the knife and scalpel were legendary throughout the great African equatorial jungles, and many a native will proudly show the scars of Dr. Schweitzer's incision. There are three days a week devoted to operations: one day for gynecological operations (usually dealing with the effects of advanced cases of gonorrhea) ; a second day for operations on tumors (the low blood count in this tropical climate makes the African unusually receptive to tumors); a third day for general surgery. On any day, additional emergency operations will be performed as needed.

The Schweitzer hospital Surgery is a wing at the end of the famed Pharmacy, but Dr. Schweitzer and his staff decided it was too small and inadequate, and a much larger surgery was planned. When I was there the foundations were already poured. I would say it is at least twice the size of the present Surgery and more modern. Hopefully, it will continue to maintain the very high percentage of successful operations. Like the smaller surgery, it will be electrified, and the putt-putt of the generator when operations are in progress will be heard.

Another aspect of the hospital brought under scrutiny has

pertained to the segregation of the races and staff. Is segregation practiced at the hospital? We must answer, emphatically, "No!" However, we must immediately point out that on the surface it often looks as though it is. There are two distinct types of Africans today. There is the sophisticated élite—often college-educated; wearing European or American type clothing; listening to records, radio, and television where possible; working at skilled industrial jobs, often as machinists or mechanics. This élite has been more-or-less "Westernized." They eat at tables, sleep on European beds, and are at home with the white staff members. They are encouraged and welcomed. However, back in the bush the African tends to live the same type of life as did his forebears. He is still a child of the jungle and is both proud of and pleased with his way of life. He has a culture—a way of living and a set of beliefs. His children may outgrow the old ways and move to the cities. Usually, this is looked upon by the older people as a calamity. There is a saying that when "The Feast of the First Fruits" comes around eventually all the city migrants will come back to their villages because tribal and family roots give a substance to their lives that the city cannot replace. Many of these tribal Africans would not be comfortable eating at the white man's table, with a knife, fork and spoon, and strange food. They prefer their own fireplaces, their own cooking methods, the chance to squat with their own people and recount tales of yesteryear and the symptoms of their illnesses without the prying ears of people whose world is different. Of course, as the meeting of the cultures continues, this too will change.

Some say that Dr. Schweitzer should have forced the meeting of the two worlds, as it is inevitable. He, on the other hand, felt that there is a self-regulatory principle at work that will bring most Africans along at the fastest rate of development that is possible without cutting them off from their roots and hence separating them from the important identification we call culture.

It is true that not many Africans come into the hospital dining room, but it is not true that there is a separate one.

Rather, there is a commissary, the reason for which we have already explained. The irony is that the missionaries have been condemned both by Africans and by Western direct-action liberals for breaking down the African's culture and westernizing him (practicing a cultural colonialism). Dr. Schweitzer was criticized for doing the opposite: accepting the values of the African culture and not undermining it. For years he was ostracized by missionaries for accepting African culture and ideas rather than trying to change them according to Western concepts. (The missionaries have, on the other hand, been criticized for a failure to appreciate the values of African culture.) Now, not only missionaries, but some politically-minded Africans, Europeans, and American liberals, in the name of equal treatment, attack Schweitzer.

An important analysis of the situation was made by Reverend Donald Szantho Harrington, minister of the Community Church of New York City, who briefly visited the Schweitzer hospital. President of the American Committee on Africa, an active leader in the civil liberties and equal rights movement, he had a perspective from both sides of the discussion for his conclusions. He wrote:

> What of the segregated staff and facilities? Yes, the African patients are housed in one building and the Europeans in another, and this appears to be segregation. But I think that one must realize that cultural differences here in Africa are very great indeed, and the motivation of the segregation becomes all important. This is not segregation for the purpose of segregation or domination, but simply and solely for the purpose of mutual comfort of the different communities. They would not be comfortable in the same kind of facilities.
>
> Perhaps Albert Schweitzer has not done enough to change the African villagers' way of life, perhaps he has not adequately encouraged them to build different kinds of villages and to learn new ways, but I think that he would answer any such charge by saying simply that one man cannot do everything, and that he came out to Africa to try to use the skills of medicine to heal the African's body

when it became sick and to teach the simplest rule of hygiene, and that someone else would have to do the revolutionary job of changing the basic African way of life.

I think I was hurt most of all by the fact that all around the table when we had our meals there was no dark face. Why has Schweitzer not been able to train some promising young African boy or girl to be a nurse or doctor? Several had become orderlies, taking temperatures, and giving shots, dispensing pharmaceuticals, etc. Why had it not been possible for African young people to be sent to France for education, and then to come back to serve their own?

I don't know whether there is any answer to this charge. Perhaps it is in this area that frustrations become too great, and the good doctor gave up too soon. I will say this, however, that the criticism of some modern Africans and Europeans ill becomes them, for they are not willing themselves to make any similar sacrifice. I was told of one African doctor from Gabon who had been trained in Paris and who came back to visit Schweitzer's Hospital. When asked whether he would take up the practice in his homeland, the Gabon, he replied indignantly, "What, come back to this dirty, filthy, poverty-stricken country! Don't you know that I have a degree from the Sorbonne, and have a good practice in Paris?"

When the time comes that an African doctor or nurse is ready to make the sacrifice as did Schweitzer himself, then there will be time for criticism, and if there is not a dark face around the staff table at Lambaréné, I have to believe it is because Albert Schweitzer simply does not know how to build the bridge to make it possible.[7]

The cultural, philosophical and theological reasons why some persons encourage and support the criticism have already been discussed, and for the most part they are unworthy of serious consideration. The criticisms themselves, however, are demanding of our attention. In the end, the answer is that the hospital has to be seen in its broader aspects and not held to

[7] Donald S. Harrington, "Three Days With Albert Schweitzer at Lambaréné," Community Church Publications, Jan. 14, 1962, 40 E. 35th St., New York, N.Y.

the preconceived attitudes which one carries with one from one's own culture. In an age of institutionalism, Dr. Schweitzer stood for the individual acting on his own motivation and according to his own insights. Indeed, when the Doctor was once asked by the Associated Press to comment on the criticism, he retorted, "Everyone is entitled to his own opinion."[8] To me he replied, "I have never felt I must answer to the crowd."

Others, however, have answered to the crowd. As we have noted already, Dr. Dana Farnsworth, Director of Medical Services at Harvard University, has written that perhaps the criticism by medical people stemmed from the pragmatic approach of Schweitzer, who, in developing a hospital "that works," ignored the codes of management for hospital administration, organization and standards—not because of a lack of standards, but because Dr. Schweitzer could not run a hospital in the jungle according to the standards of a New York City hospital. One of the clearest examples of this was given in the *Iowa Alumni Review* of February 1961, published by the State University of Iowa Alumni Association. Professor Hans Ulrich Zellweger, M.D., Research Professor of Pediatrics at the University of Iowa, recalled in an article the two years he spent on the staff of the Schweitzer hospital. Discussing the pros and cons of the medical quality of the hospital, he summarized with these paragraphs:

> That Schweitzer succeeded as well as he has in treating the natives, I believe, is part of the practical yielding to reality that is part of Schweitzer's makeup. He made concessions to native custom. He practiced his healing in terms the natives could understand; and went as far as he could without deviating from the principles of modern medicine. This is apparent in the physical setup of the hospital.
>
> Of the twenty different tribes in the Gabon area which his hospital serves, some of them openly war with each other, and nearly all are distrustful of each other. Even persons outside of a single family group are regarded with suspicion.

[8] *Boston Herald,* January 5, 1964.

Schweitzer took this into account, and set up a barracks for each tribe.

Inside the family group, however, ties are very close, and this posed another problem. It would have been difficult to separate a patient from his family. The sick man would arrive at the hospital with his whole family—sometimes several wives and a whole raft of children. They would all be housed in the same barracks as the patient. It was not unusual to see one or two small children sleeping around the extension apparatus for a fractured leg.

In the case of contagious disease, however, Schweitzer set up ironclad rules. Strict measures were taken to make the natives conform. For patients with amoebic dysentery, for example, Schweitzer built an enclosure with a few huts and a garden, where the patients were locked in until they were dequarantined. Likewise, patients who were undergoing a vermifuge (treatment to expel intestinal parasites and worms) were locked in for the duration of the treatment.

The food we handed out to the patients was uncooked and unprepared, and consisted of bananas, manoc, dry fish and salt. (Salt is a great luxury.) The natives would not have accepted prepared meals. They superstitiously believed that all sorts of witchcraft could be mixed into the food. Therefore, each family had a small fire in front of the barracks where they cooked their own meals.

This naturally gives a hospital a primitive appearance, which has often come into criticism. The living conditions and sleeping and eating facilities were purposely adjusted to the native style of life. There is no point in giving a native a pillow, if he has been used to putting his head on a stone all his life. The natives felt much more at ease by finding living conditions similar to those at home. And hygienic standards were still maintained. They were kept simple, of course, and their simplicity made them efficient. I have since worked in other hospitals in other countries under similar conditions, where primitive people came into contact with complicated modern hospital facilities. The clash of extremes was ludicrous, sometimes disastrous, confusion resulting from this can be overcome sometimes by complicated organization, requiring a large staff. This kind of staff was not available in Lambaréné.

A more recent physician and surgeon on the staff at the Schweitzer hospital has been Robert M. Goldwyn, M.D., Harvey Cushing Fellow in Surgery, Peter Bent Brigham Hospital, Boston, Massachusetts. To most people he is best known for the famed surgical cases in which he has re-united severed arms to the human body in recent years. His medical skill is therefore well-known and he ranks with the outstanding surgeons of our time. He spent over two months on the hospital staff in Lambaréné in 1960, and has recently written an article concerning his analysis of the medical situation in the light of criticism.[9]

Dr. Goldwyn writes that Schweitzer did not oppose indictments of his work because they violated his privacy. He points out that Schweitzer welcomed visitors graciously, even when it was known they were critical of his efforts, and always allowed them complete access to the hospital and its personnel. Of course, Dr. Goldwyn admits that the criticisms do hint of some truth, but adds that they are "enormously distorted." Many of the criticisms, he suggests, are like those of a panel of city doctors reviewing the practices of a ninety-year-old rural family physician. They would find his methods not the latest; his knowledge not the most complete; and his office and equipment not the most modern. Yet "his desire to help and his efforts would still be useful." A public attack on him would be decidedly unfair, particularly if "the hypercritical doctors returned to their homes after having left the old practitioner alone to care for his patients."

Continuing, Dr. Goldwyn gives this description: "About 70 buildings now constitute what he has called his 'jungle clinic,' and it is truly a monument to one man's tenacity and ingenuity. Those of us who mow the lawn on a hot summer day and secretly expect a Purple Heart can scarcely imagine the difficulties Dr. Schweitzer had to overcome in order to build his hospital in the jungle." This might even have required Schweitzer to be stubborn and authoritarian, he suggests, as well as frugal. For all these qualities, Schweitzer has been

[9] *The Register-Leader,* January, 1965; UUA, 25 Beacon Street, Boston, Mass.

condemned. Then Dr. Goldwyn gives us this description:

The medical conditions most frequently treated at the Albert Schweitzer hospital are malaria, leprosy, gonorrhea, tuberculosis, rheumatic heart disease, dysentery, filariasis, and parasitic infestations. Whatever drugs and medications that are needed are usually available. One of the most interesting features of the disease pattern at Lambaréné is the absence of many of our common entities: appendicitis, cholecystitus, peptic ulcer, cancer of the breast and gut, coronary artery disease, and peripheral arterial insufficiency.

Now 89, Dr. Schweitzer does not operate and only occasionally sees patients, although he is usually informed about serious cases and complications. The critics who claim that Dr. Schweitzer does not know his medicine and seldom personally treated his patients are absolutely wrong. Many times I and other members of the medical staff consulted him, and his judgement always proved correct. While he may not know the techniques of open-heart surgery, he can certainly deal adequately with any medical problem coming to his hospital. One should remember that Dr. Schweitzer performed most of the surgery during the World War II years (he was then 68) and his painstaking detailed operative notes can still be seen in the old log books.

That Dr. Schweitzer's hospital could be improved in terms of comforts is undeniable. So, perhaps, could Dr. Schweitzer have a more comfortable dwelling rather than the two small cluttered rooms that adjoin those of his staff. He forgets about comforts both for himself and for others who live with him. If he were more mindful of physical ease, he would never have gone to Africa.

Because of their own deficiencies, many of Dr. Schweitzer's critics are still seeking the perfect father figure. They blame him for lacking qualities which he has never professed to have. In his many writings, he has stressed the personal motives and circumstances of his decision to go to Africa. He was actively and humanely concerned about Africa and its people before most of the world was. Now it is the fashion. That his thinking about Africa is not like that of a younger man of today is certainly true. He readily admits this as well as the fact that his hospital is not perfect, and that he could make many changes. He has not taken in his sails, however, and at this moment continues to build and to improve the hospital.

Oftentimes, we must recall that some doctors, including those who have criticized Dr. Schweitzer, are not as good as they should be. Our hospitals in the United States are not always efficient. Indeed, some of the most famous and highly regarded, with untold resources, suffer for lack of adequate personnel, facilities, scheduling, and human love toward the patient. Doctors and reporters who single out the Schweitzer establishment, built far from the resources of civilization, facing hazards unknown in industrial countries or metropolitan areas, may well ponder whether they are able themselves to bring a similar peace of mind to every sick person and his family, and to give so much confidence, as Dr. Schweitzer and his hospital have generated. In addition, the Schweitzer hospital has had an amazingly good rate of post-operative recovery, better than that of most hospitals. In a paper studying the surgical records of 450 cases in 1960, Dr. Robert M. Goldwyn and Dr. Richard L. Friedman reported in the *New England Journal of Medicine,* May 18, 1961, that the operative mortality was only 0.44 per cent—actually only two deaths, one due to a myocardial infarct (heart trouble) and the other due to pneumonia. All 450 cases studied would be called major surgery cases in the United States.

Accordingly, we cannot escape the conclusion that in his primitive hospital, without most modern conveniences and comforts, a good medical record and useful service was supplied by Dr. Schweitzer and the team of doctors, nurses and orderlies who worked with him.

Chapter 10

SCHWEITZER'S CHALLENGE TO SOCIETY

In the realm of ideas, Albert Schweitzer was among the most articulate of individuals. He was a social thinker, a student of comparative religions and cultures, and an interpreter of civilization and of human destiny. As such, this man, often called a universal genius, spoke out against the present course of civilization. He was an audacious challenger of nationalism, institutionalism, conformity, unthought out solutions, and superficiality in cultural and human affairs. He was one of the greatest free minds of our day and was properly identified as a liberal in the best meaning of that term.

It is somewhat amazing that so challenging and disconcerting a commentator on the social scene became popular. Although Dr. Schweitzer did not reflect in his philosophical writings the prevalent ideas of the great masses of people, he was beloved and supported because people saw in him a modern man who actually practiced the religion of love.

That his religious beliefs differed from the common did not occur to most. In consequence, when he was "exposed" as holding ideas that were not popular, or when his motivations were challenged, many good people were shocked.

Dr. Schweitzer went to Africa not to "bear the white man's burden" to the "fuzzy wuzzy" but to repudiate the colonialism of which Kipling sang. He went not to "lesser breeds without the law" but to people who were imposed on by the white man. He may have been one of the world's first great anticolonialists; it is a paradox that such a possibility is not recognized today by people who continue to attack him.

As one peruses his writings, one is impressed over and over by the magnitude of Schweitzer's challenge and critique of unthinking modern life. For Schweitzer, thought was the essential means to the solving of problems and the righting of old shortcomings or failures. Today's culture, however, relies greatly upon catchwords and slogans, hidden persuaders, manipulation psychologists, emotional herd-feeling, and conformity, all of which obstruct individual reflection. Consequently, many seem to govern their lives, their deliberate actions, and their outlooks, by irrational or antirational impulses. Herd man—civilized man—appears to be moving closer to irrationality than have former generations.

What a relief to look back upon the age of the Enlightenment or upon the great classical ages when men exalted reason! Schweitzer, perhaps the last of the Enlightenment minds, although born a century later, was always true to the principles of reason, naturalism and thought. Those elements combined to make not only his religion but his culture. For his ethical imperative he went back to Jesus of Nazareth, but he found the motive power of the Stoics more helpful than that of Christianity. Consequently, his was a many-sided dissent from modern civilization; he tried to recreate the conditions for a rational civilization.

Concerning the relationship of man's thought to the life he lives and the universe in which he lives, Schweitzer wrote: "All thinking must renounce the attempt to explain the universe. What is glorious in it is united with what is full of horror. What is full of meaning is united with what is senseless. The spirit of the universe is at once creative and destructive—it creates what it destroys and destroys what it creates, and therefore it remains to us a riddle. And we must inevitably resign ourselves to this."

Schweitzer thus embarked, years ago, on a most daring avenue of modern thought in his renunciation of an affirmative world view. He was forced to the logical conclusion that the universe itself was morally, rationally and objectively neutral and that it remained for man to take sides and to make life meaningful, to make life moral, to make life rational, to make life consistent.

While Schweitzer carved out a road which the Existentialists were to follow, he found the ethical too compelling to allow him to stop, as they did, without arriving at meaning and purpose. Meaning and purpose he found in the will to live. Only a great encyclopedic thinker of the stature of Schweitzer could convincingly have cut his way through the accumulated knowledge of the race to arrive at that simple conclusion—and to arrive at it from rational grounds rather than out of ignorance.

Schweitzer was at home in the intellectual systems and ideologies of the East as well as the West. Eastern thought, he found, offered more to our understanding of the world view than did Western thought. However, it was valuable only in its explanations, for it failed to offer any motivations for accepting this life. It moved from passivity to negation and became a life-destructive philosophy.

After exploring Eastern thought, Dr. Schweitzer returned to the Stoics and to Jesus for the ethical imperative. The Eastern systems were world- and life-negating, whereas what he was seeking was an affirmation of the world and life. And he had to end with an affirmation growing out of a rational, rather than a supernatural, ethical system. Thus, Schweitzer's dissent in philosophy and ethics tied in rather closely with his dissent against nationalism, colonialism and militarism.

His need for a rational ethic was also carried over to his dissent against the established orthodoxy of western religions, since thought, rather than faith, had become primary for him. Reading Oswald Spengler's *Decline of the West* as a student, Dr. Schweitzer had found Spengler's ideas "without substance" and decided some day to write a book of his own on the process of decay and disintegration in society. With the coming of World War I to Europe, when the decline of civilization was not only noticeable, but accelerated, he could put off writing his book no longer. Accordingly, during four months of house arrest, he spent most of his time writing the first volume of the *Philosophy of Civilization.*[1]

Dr. Schweitzer for many years realized that his generation's optimism, which had stressed perpetual progress or, as it was put, "the progress of mankind onward and upward forever," was shallow and unreliable. That optimism, he believed, needed hardheaded examination, for it did not take into account the essential drive necessary if society was creatively and constructively to meet its problems.

In 1915 Dr. Schweitzer suddenly realized that he was becoming too despondent about the future of society. Why not consider the constructive features and the hopes for the future?

He turned, then, from Spengler to Schopenhauer and Nietzsche, balancing their propositions with those of Kant and the German Idealists. Of course, his Enlightenment studies were brought to bear, as well.

He sought to avoid the absurdities he found in European philosophy and to correct the negation of the Oriental philosophies. The main point of philosophical inquiry for Schweitzer, however, was for the pragmatic purpose of aiding man to face the question of his place and role in the universe.

"Civilization can only revive when there shall come into being in a number of individuals a new tone of mind independent of the one prevalent among the crowd and in opposition to it, a tone of mind which will gradually win influence over the collective one, and in the end determine its character."[2] The hope for civilization was the creation of a tone of mind which had to be developed personally by the individual.

Schweitzer found one clear sign in his preparation for *The Quest of the Historical Jesus,* as he considered Ernest Renan, a great nineteenth-century French Rationalist. As a young man, Renan had been one of the first to make full use of the historical criticism of the Gospels, which led to his rejection of the Gospels as historically accurate or reliable. Schweitzer discovered that Renan's conclusion had stood in the way of further creative scholarship; it had paralyzed Renan's

1 *Out of My Life and Thought,* p. 172 ff.

2 *Ibid.,* p. 278 ff.

thought, forcing him to become a defender of revolutionary positions already reached.

Dr. Schweitzer, seeing himself in the somewhat analogous position of rejecting established dogma, decided that thought itself could not be allowed to become a straitjacket that would constrict his mind. Like Renan, he recognized that he was estranged from the larger community of the church; but unlike Renan, he did not become trapped by his estrangement. As he told Norman Cousins, "I think I can understand how Renan's work affected him when he didn't allow it to redefine his life for him. This is what I mean when I say I came to Lambaréné because I wanted to make my life my argument. I didn't want my ideas to become an end in themselves."[3]

Having arrived at his position, Dr. Schweitzer remained an incorrigible individualist. His position on ethics, expressed in the concept of Reverence for Life, was one example. His position against warfare and nuclear fallout was another. His internationalism was part of his nonconformity, as was his religious liberalism.

In writing of Christian truth, for instance, he called attention forcefully to its enshrinement of falsehood rather than honesty: "In what a condition we find ourselves today, merely because in the earliest Christian period writings were allowed to appear, bearing quite falsely the names of apostles, in order to give greater authority to the ideas put forth in them! They have been for generations of Christians a source of painful dissension."[4]

He even discussed the capability of Jesus to err, something that most churchmen would not allow themselves to consider: "What can we do in the face of what stands clearly recorded in the Gospels? Are we acting in the spirit of Jesus if we attempt with hazardous and sophisticated explanations to force the sayings into agreement with the dogmatic teachings of His absolute and universal incapability of error. He Himself never made any claim to such omniscience. . . . Knowledge of

[3] Cousins, *op. cit.,* p. 195 ff.
[4] Schweitzer, *Op. cit.,* pp. 52-53.

spiritual truth is not called upon to prove its genuineness by showing further knowledge about the events of world history and matters of ordinary life. Its province lies on a quite different level from the latter's, and it is quite independent of it."[5]

In an article published in the 1920's, entitled "The Relations of the White and Coloured Races," he gave this clean-cut explanation:

> I wish to discuss colonization, and the relations of the white and coloured races which it involves, as a peasant talks of his cabbages, and not as an artist or a poet would depict the same cabbages. . . . . Let us concentrate upon the essential problem of colonization, which is the conservation and protection and the exercise of the rights of man.
>
> The idea of the rights of man was formed and developed in the eighteenth century, when society was an organized and stable thing. Whatever the fundamental rights of man are, they can only be fully secured in a stable and well-ordered society. In a disordered society the very well-being of man himself often demands that his fundamental rights should be abridged. We have, then, to start in our discussion from an empirical rather than a philosophical basis.
>
> The fundamental rights of man are, first, the right to habitation; secondly, the right to move freely; thirdly, the right to the soil and subsoil, and to the use of it; fourthly, the right to freedom of labour and of exchange; fifthly, the right to justice; sixthly, the right to live within a natural, national organization; and, seventhly, the right to education. We now ask ourselves how far are these safeguarded by existing colonization?
>
> The power to safeguard the rights of man varies in direct relation with the social order. If the social order is normal, the rights can be complete; but if it is abnormal, they are menaced and limited.[6]

More recently, despite the necessity for white men to re-

[5] *Ibid.*, pp. 57-58.

[6] Reprinted in George Seaver's *Albert Schweitzer: The Man and His Mind*, Harper, as an Appendix.

main silent, he spoke in behalf of allowing the Africans to solve their own problems, noting that black colonialism (exploitation of one African territory by another) was as reprehensible as white colonialism. He wrote to a Belgian newspaper:

> My advice . . . is that of an Old Africa hand who has been living for almost fifty years in an area near the Congo. . . . The era of colonialism does not exist any more, and the colonial empire of the Congo does not exist any more either. Surviving are only two pieces of this empire formed by people and tribes. . . . Neither has any claim on the other. Neither has any obligations toward the other. They are absolutely independent of one another. No war, undertaken by one against the other to suppress it has any judicial foundation. . . . It is incomprehensible that a foreign state would be presently in a state of war with Katanga to compel it to pay royalties to the other Congolese state.
>
> No foreign state can claim the right to compel one of these two independent states to submit to the other. . . . The United Nations associates itself with that foreign country and in this undertaking runs the risk of losing the well-deserved respect which they enjoy in the world. The mission of the United Nations is not to wage war.[7]

It is perhaps in the perspective of Schweitzer's challenge to the status quo that attacks on him are best understood—the individualist who refuses to conform, whether in social, political, professional or on medical terms. We see that challenge in many ways, including his efforts to arouse world opinion against nuclear warfare and testing; his refusal to align himself either with colonialism or native independence movements; and his disdain of rigid medical codes for hospital administration in favor of pragmatic decisions. In all those areas—intellectual, cultural and professional—Schweitzer was independent. Such a person is a jolting disparity in a world of conformities.

[7] *La Dernière Heure,* Brussels, Belgium, September 18, 1962.

Chapter 11

MY LIFE MY ARGUMENT

In contemplating the life of Dr. Schweitzer, certain significant features stand out. As he once replied to Henry Clark, in Oslo, "Read my books. No one can express the ideas of a man as well as he has expressed them himself in his writings."[1] This we have attempted to do: to show his life through his thoughts—to quote copiously from his words and from the words of those close enough to him to have been significantly touched by his insight—in order to bring it into perspective for us. "No man is ever completely and permanently a stranger to his fellow-man. Man belongs to man. Man has claims on man."[2] This sense of our involvement with one another, and of the deeper ties of human community, were the essence of the faith which Norman Cousins so ably expressed in his account of Dr. Schweitzer's decision to go to Africa, ending in the determination: "I decided I would make my life my argument." As Dr. Schweitzer said to Dr. Greeley and me, "I am only a person trying to live his religion." He brought thought and life into juxtaposition so that they complement and exist only in one another. He showed us that life is the fulfillment of thought and that thought is the basis of life. This consistency made Schweitzer that which he gloried in: a rational being.

Rationalism leads to ethics, however, and if life does not fulfill thought, than it becomes irrational. Consequently, for

[1] Henry Clark, *The Ethical Mysticism of Albert Schweitzer*, Boston, Beacon, 1962, Preface.

[2] Anderson and Exman, *op. cit.*, p. 98.

Dr. Schweitzer, the highest form of life was the ethical and rational being, and it was this that he personified. He, because he was ethical, became the concerned man, thus the involved man. "Man belongs to man. Man has claims on man." The solution to man's problems may be as simple as this: the very unselfishness Schweitzer personified—the sense of participation one in another, even to "the fellowship of those who bear the mark of pain."[3]

Indeed, Schweitzer himself expressed this in various ways. In his first interview on world affairs following World War II, he told Melvin Arnold and Charles R. Joy:

> We must substitute the power of understanding and truth that is really true, for propaganda; [we must substitute] a noble kind of patriotism which aims at ends that are worthy of mankind, for the patriotism current today; [we must substitute] a humanity with a common civilization; for idolized nationalisms, [we must substitute] a restored faith in the civilized state, for a society which lacks true idealism . . . . a faith in the possibility of progress, for a mentality stripped of all spirituality. These are our tasks.[4]

From this position he moved on to the larger discussion of individual responsibility for the mass murder of atomic war, which led to the award to him of the Nobel Peace Prize in 1953 for his significant contribtution. In back of his motivation still, however, was *individual* action, not group action. He remained, thus, to many socially conscious and concerned persons, the enigma of our day: an individual taking a stand rather than an integral member of an organized movement.

Dr. Schweitzer's testament was the power of the individual, of the rational, ethical person confronting the issues of life and having a concern for them.

This, even today, touches off criticism of Dr. Schweitzer and his hospital. Yet his hospital stands as a monument to one

[3] *On the Edge of the Primeval Forest,* p. 116.

[4] C. R. Joy and Melvin Arnold, *The Africa of Albert Schweitzer,* New York, Harper, 1948.

man's concern. Consider some of the specialized features of this hospital. Those critical of the hospital must admit that it is medically sound even when they attack its "primitive conditions." For instance, *Time* wrote: "Schweitzer's institution has a good medical record, and the city's Europeans generally choose it over the new government hospital. Few hospitals anywhere can offer such a dedicated staff, or one that lives as austerely. . . . The old man stubbornly refuses to go modern. Says he: 'Circumstances demand that the hospital be primitive in keeping with the primitive state of the people'."[5] *Time's* account, which was critical, called Schweitzer "an anachronism," but had to admit, as do all objective criticisms, that the hospital has a good medical record, its staff is superior, and its therapy modern, no matter how much one may be dismayed at what has often been described as "primitive village conditions."

Besides its good medical record and surgical practices, there are three aspects of the hospital which make it somewhat unique. The first does not really belong to our concept of a hospital at all: the orphanage. Yet what does one do with an orphan or foundling children where there is no Red Feather Agency? In the Schweitzer Hospital, they are kept and provided for until someone offers them a home or they grow up. Readers of Dr. Schweitzer's books will recall that boys are regarded as bad luck and as economic liabilities. Poor families with more problems and burdens than they can cope with are the same the world over. Sometimes the burdens of the African parents were too heavy, and they would desert a newborn child or bring it in and leave it on the kindly old doctor's "doorstep," as it were—a youngster they could no longer care for but would entrust to le grand Docteur and his ministering angels. Thus, without plan or desire, an orphanage became a regular part of the hospital. Then, there were (and still are) the conditions of violence in the jungle. A family would be set upon by an animal, or by an invasion of ants, beast or men. Miraculously, a baby would sometimes escape.

[5] *Time* Magazine, June 21, 1963, p. 35.

When the screaming infant would be discovered by passing natives who knew nothing of the family connections of the child, they would bring it to the hospital. It would become a ward of the Doctor's until, hopefully, someone could identify its tribe or family.

The hospital has no school, but fortunately it is located near two mission schools—the Catholic, across the river, and the Protestant, down the shoreline at the juncture of a branch stream with the Ogowe. Youngsters could walk to the Protestant mission or be canoed to the Catholic mission. With Dr. Schweitzer, it was not a matter of religious preference where the children were educated: it was a matter of grades and room only. Whichever mission could take them in did so. In the Doctor's time, while most of the children walked to the Protestant mission, enough of them went to the Catholic mission to upset certain religious institutionalists who felt that Dr. Schweitzer was not being sufficiently loyal to his own Protestant mission beginnings. Possibly this, as well as anything, emphasized Dr. Schweitzer's universality of mind, and showed him to be a man above the lesser sectarian battles of our time.

The Leper Village is another splendid and unique aspect of the Schweitzer hospital. It is a village set apart, completely rebuilt with the funds from the Nobel Peace Prize. Here are modern, trim bungalows, the finest dwellings at the hospital. The Leper Village will accommodate two hundred lepers. When I visited it, there were one hundred and sixty adult lepers with twenty children making up the village. The children were delightful, and I was particularly glad my wife had stuffed my shoes and suitcase corners with balloons and lollypops. The doctor in charge was the Japanese medic, Doctor Isao Takabashi, a modern-day saint. With his European and African nurses, he carried on a remarkable program.

"Your American drugs now cure leprosy," Dr. Takabashi explained, "but the African does not understand it is cured. He recalls the long history of retarded cases that broke out at a later time and infected others. Accordingly, African superstition says a Leper is accursed, and one who deals with him will be cursed. Therefore, even after cure, many lepers must stay here because they will not be accepted back in the villages. Dr. Schweitzer wants us to make it clear that they will always have a home here, and even if they do go out, they can return any time they need to."

Looking at the lepers who live here—often with resignation and peaceful demeanor, dismembered by leprosy in the days before cures were possible—one recognizes the value of the Doctor's program that provides a home, with freedom, for these unfortunates. Also, one catches a glimpse of the wonders now possible through the miracles of science. To contemplate that such stubbed arms and legs can be prevented from occurring in the future is indeed an uplifting experience.

The psychiatric wards at the hospital are another example of the advancement seen in this institution. There was no psychiatrist on the hospital staff, but Dr. Schweitzer kept a psychiatrically-trained registered nurse on the staff who, under his supervision, was able to work with the mentally disturbed patients brought to the hospital. He supervised this aspect of the hospital's medical treatment more closely than others and was proud of the record here. Patients were not confined, but were allowed greater freedom than is usual. "Tender, loving care, consideration, and patience" are the three elements the Schweitzer therapy stressed. "How do the mental patients come?" we asked.

"Usually they are brought in by their families, or by the village or tribal elders."

"What are their problems?" we queried.

"They are usually unable to communicate or relate to the family, village or tribal patterns any longer."

Then Dr. Schweitzer and the nurses explained that the tribes and family clans are remarkably adept at bringing back to reality persons suffering from any minor mental disorders, but that there is a point beyond which they cannot give help. When they feel they have reached this point, they bring the unfortunate into the hospital. No time limit is placed on the length of time allowed for a patient. They may spend the rest of their lives there if they do not respond, but this is not usually necessary. If it is, the hospital is prepared to care for them as long as they live.

The most interesting person in the mental wards was not confined at all. She was lovingly known as "Madame Sans Nom," (sometimes called "Momma Sans Nom"), a dwarfed aborigine who made her way into the hospital compound several years ago jabbering incoherent sounds which many thought to be an unknown tongue. She was without communication with others for several years and was personally and totally isolated. She wore no clothing when she arrived except a G-string, and since then she has never donned any. Through the G-string she wore a long knife. She carried a spear, and ate earth and worms, occasionally some fruit. Now and then she would feel gay and put on a dance; at other times she was quite determined to be left alone. She was a beloved creature at the hospital then, and both patients and staff speculated about her.

One theory was that she was a mentally ill person, paranoid, unable to relate to the society about her or place herself in her world meaningfully.

Others suggested that she was the last survivor of one of the more primitive earth-eating tribes of the interior, who, following the demise of the last of her tribe, made her way westward until she found a place to stop, at the Schweitzer hospital. Here she was able to live on the fringe of a native culture she could observe and enjoy, but in which she could not participate.

There were variations of these two theories, some suggesting that she underwent a traumatic experience when her family or village perished through an epidemic or some other type of catastrophe, and that subsequently she became reduced to a near-animal existence, grubbing for food and muttering gibberish. Aborigine or paranoid, however, the mental ward was her home, and the kindness and patience of the nurses helped her to feel she was one of them, although she never ventured inside a building, living her entire life out-of-doors.

These various types of personal medical ministrations indicate the broader concern of this unique hospital. One example of the personal aspect of Dr. Schweitzer's management of the hospital is reported in Everett Skillings' "Postscript," added to the second American edition of *Out of My Life and Thought,* published in 1949. Mr. Skillings gives us this account:

> In February 1934, Schweitzer is again in Europe spending the spring and summer, for the most part at Günsbach working upon the third volume of his Philosophy and upon the preparation of the Gifford Lectures. In that year Dr. Ernest Bueding . . . came in contact with Schweitzer under very interestng circumstances at the Pasteur Institute in Paris. He relates an incident which is characteristic of the Doctor's noble spirit and attitude toward medicine: "A group of research workers were engaged in preparing and studying a vaccine against yellow fever. They succeeded in obtaining a preparation which offered some degree of immunity. One day someone called from Colmar, Alsace, requesting information about this vaccine. He indicated that he would like to take it to Africa in order to vaccinate some patients in a hospital, as well as some other natives. When informed that serious side reactions may occur as a result of the administration of this vaccine, he said that he would only consider large scale vaccinations if he himself were first given this preparation in order to experience and evaluate any untoward effects. He was asked about his age and when he said he was about sixty, the person in charge advised strongly not to try this preparation himself. This was to no avail and the 'doctor from Colmar' replied that he would come to Paris the next day in order to discuss the matter further. He insisted that if the vaccine is considered safe enough for the natives of Africa, it should be safe enough for him. When this telephone conversation was discussed I happened to be in the laboratory and I immediately wondered whether the 'doctor from Colmar' was not Dr. Schweitzer whose books had inspired my greatest admiration. My guess proved to be correct and I explained as well as possible the great personality, the ideas, and the achievements of Dr. Schweitzer before his arrival the next morning. When he reached the laboratory, the chief of the

> latter tried again to convince him that it would be unwise to try this experiment on himself. However, this was again unsuccessful; he was determined to have the vaccination performed. As a measure of precaution he was hospitalized for two days at the Hospital Pasteur. Fortunately, Dr. Schweitzer had no serious reactions from the injection. However, he was a very 'bad patient' because he could not see why these precautions of keeping him inactive in the hospital for two days should be taken."[6]

The consistency of Dr. Schweitzer's own life was highly individualistic with him. This was part of the fascination of the man. Yet the consistency was from the soul outward to the ethical response: from the mind outward to the affirmation. Does one have a right to expose his soul and examine it? Schweitzer, seemingly, says not. He wrote: "A man must not try to force his way into the personality of another. To analyse others—unless it be to help back to sound mind someone in spiritual and intellectual confusion—is a rude commencement, for there is a modesty of the soul which we must recognize, just as we do that of the body. The soul too has its clothing of which we must not deprive it, and no one has a right to say to another: 'Because we belong to each other as we do, I have a right to know your thoughts.' Not even a mother can treat her child in that way."[7]

However, we are fortunate, for Dr. Schweitzer's writings have given us many clues to his inner life and thought, those which he was willing for us to see. In the Epilogue to *Out of My Life and Thought,* he exposes his soul and thinking in a clear view. He opens by saying:

> Two perceptions cast their shadows over my existence. One consists in my realization that the world is inexplicably mysterious and full of suffering; the other in the fact that I have been born into a period of spiritual decadence in mankind. I have become familiar with and ready to deal with each through the thinking which has led me to the

[6] *Out of My Life and Thought,* 1949 ed., pp. 251-52.
[7] *Memoirs of Childhood and Youth,* pp. 110-12.

> ethical world and life-affirmation of Reverence for Life. In that principle my life has found a firm footing and a clear path to follow.[8]

He was reminiscent of the old liberal intellectuals. He wrote, "I therefore stand in the world as one who aims at making men less shallow and morally better by making them think."[9] Thus he exposed the entire import of his witness and challenge to mankind. He sought to stimulate us to become rational and ethical beings. In doing so, he knew that he had set himself against "the entire spirit of our age." He also wrote that "renunciation of thinking is a declaration of spiritual bankruptcy. Where there is no longer a conviction that men can get to know the truth by their own thinking, skepticism has begun." For some, the escape is through authoritarianism, but he warned us: "But the acceptance of authoritative truth, even if that truth has both spiritual and ethical content, does not bring skepticism to an end; it merely covers it up." The only hope for man is truth discoverable by himself. "Our spiritual life is rotten throughout because it is permeated through and through with skepticism, and we live, in consequence, in a world which in every respect is full of falsehood. We are not far from shipwreck on the rock of wanting to have every truth organized."[10] The type of elemental thinking found in Reverence for Life, and in Stoicism, has much to commend it to the modern age, but because these are contrary to the spirit of over-organization and conformity, they are passed over by nearly all. The "fundamental truth of Stoicism is true, namely, that man must bring himself into a spiritual relation with the world, and become one with it. In its essence, Stoicism is a nature-philosophy that ends in mysticism."[11]

The church must come to terms with elemental thinking.

[8] *Out of My Life and Thought,* p. 254.
[9] *Ibid.*
[10] *Ibid.,* pp. 258-259.
[11] *Ibid.,* p. 261.

He wrote: "If Christianity, for the sake of any tradition or for any considerations whatever, refuses to have itself interpreted in terms of ethico-religious thinking, it will be a misfortune for itself and for mankind."[12]

He continues the passage by saying that "My hope is that the emergence of an elemental mode of thought, which may lead us to the ethico-religious idea of Reverence for Life, may contribute to the bringing of Christianity and thought closer to each other."[13]

Examining his own position, as we have noted, Dr. Schweitzer wrote that he was a pessimist so far as his knowledge went, but in his willing and hoping he was an optimist. He also held a unique position in another way: he stood out as one of the company of great men who stand alone, and therein he carried a great estrangement which severed him from the mass of humanity. Just as other great men by their offices—A President or an ecclesiastical leader, (i.e., Bishop) for instance—may always be surrounded by others; nevertheless they are separated from the throngs about them. They walk amid millions, but alone. So, in his own limited way, did Dr. Schweitzer. His Lambaréné hospital became a crossroads thronged with people; he was surrounded, yet was alone, a deeply reflective man whose thought, sympathies and vision were not in the present company or moment. For instance, he was a Christian minister, but was separated from close relationships with the other clergy by his marriage to a Jewish woman. He was a great exponent of rational ethics during a time when the world preferred to act by political expediency. He was an exemplar of Christian love, but was often excluded from Christian communion due to his doctrinal variation. He created one of the most affirmative examples of medicine-in-action, but doctors sometimes shied away from admitting that he was an example of good modern medical practice. In spite of this lack of consistency with external institutions, persons and situations, however, he was nonetheless a highly con-

[12] *Ibid.*, p. 278.
[13] *Ibid.*

sistent person, albeit a complex one. Through his consistency, however, the complexity made sense.

In Schweitzer we have had one of the most complex natures of our time: a man of faith and action, yet a man who was a dissenter against the establishment; a pessimist who nevertheless continued to build; a critic, yet a creator. He worked nearly five decades with the colonial government, yet he never became *persona non grata.* He lived a lifetime in Africa, soothing the pain, tenderly nursing the bodies and quieting the minds of hurt and frantic African patients, yet he never counseled them to throw off their chains. It appeared to the superficial that he survived through a negative device of not speaking, not acting, and not leading; yet he was silent only in non-constructive ways so that he could perform the constructive services which were open to him.

It is easy for those who follow Schweitzer to Africa, a half century later, to pose as leaders. It is easy a half century after he was pledged to be as "mute as a fish" to articulate the twentieth century demands of freedom. Little do such critics realize that only the patient toilers like Schweitzer opened up and prepared the way, creating a world conscience of dignity and respect for the African. All we can surmise now is that Schweitzer knew; he held to a counsel of patience, knowing that civilization would inexorably bring demands for freedom which could not be avoided. Those who challenge, however, say, "but why did he remain silent?" The answer is obvious. Today belongs to the African. The white man cannot endure in Africa—with its uneasy plebiscites and alliances—if he does not accept the conditions of silence. It is too late for any white man to speak out in Africa in the nineteen sixties.

Schweitzer made his life his argument. Words can no longer speak for him: only a half-century of committed African service. This should be enough.

Chapter 12

Epilogue

SCHWEITZER AT NINETY

On Dr. Schweitzer's ninetieth birthday many persons around the world stopped to pay respects to him. Others gathered at the riverside in Lambaréné to honor him. Still others thought that outside of the ability to endure, the honors and respect were not deserved. At ninety, Dr. Schweitzer did not receive the same unanimity of acclaim that he did at eighty, seventy, or sixty. In earlier days there were far fewer voices to belittle him, and few dared insinuate that his acclaim was overrated. Yet, by the same token, his name was probably not so much of a household word around the world that it is today, and in earlier days fewer were the heads of state, governments and worldwide agencies who took note of his birthdays. President Lyndon B. Johnson, for instance, wrote him from the United States: "It is the good fortune of all men everywhere that you have lived among us for ninety years. In your commitment to truth and service you have touched and deepened the lives of millions you have never met. On behalf of the American people I salute you."

The *Washington Post* editorialized on his birthday that sometime in the future there must be a "Quest for the Historical Albert Schweitzer," paraphrasing the title of his most famous theological book, *Quest for the Historical Jesus.*

We are perhaps too close to his last year to bring it all into historical perspective. Following a period in which there was more bitter and highly controversial criticism of Dr. Schweitzer than in any other period of his life, we might begin to sketch an historical perspective so that future biographers and historians will have access to the context of the controversy as seen at this time. Like a whirlwind, it had blown about his feet and reputation during his last year. On his ninetieth birthday, he allowed himself the brief luxury of a reminiscence. Attempts had been made to tarnish his name, to discredit his hospital, to challenge his position on African affairs; and it had been suggested that his life has been over-evaluated. Writers, critics, and debunkers tried to pick an argument with him, but he had gone silently on his way, minding only the day-to-day business of his hospital. Now, on his ninetieth birthday, he finally spoke out.

"Africans themselves showed me the way," he told a hushed audience of about fifty persons gathered at his birthday breakfast. "At first I wanted to build a hospital like those in Europe. But Africans—two simple laborers—convinced me that here the conditions are different. I have built an African hospital for Africans."

With this he was silent once more. He would not be drawn into controversy. Let others charge that he sat on foam rubber cushions while his guests sat on hard wood; let others charge that he ate an egg a day while others ate oatmeal—must he defend a slight consideration for diet at ninety while he still worked a full twelve hour day? Would one dare suggest that in his tiny cluttered room, with an iron cot for a bed, he coddled himself in the midst of luxury? It seemed that this was inferred, but he would not answer such charges.

Years ago he had written: "I must forgive lies directed against me because so many times my own conduct has been blotted by lies. I must forgive the lovelessness, the hatred, the slander, the fraud, the arrogance which I encounter, since I myself have so often lacked love, and have hated, slandered, defrauded, and been arrogant, and I must forgive without noise or fuss. In general, I do not succeed in forgiving fully; I do not even get as far as being always just. But he who tries to live by this principle, simple and hard as it is, will know the real adventures and triumphs of the soul."[1]

His point of view prized the privacy of the individual. He wrote: "I think, therefore, that no one should compel himself to show to others more of his inner life than he feels it natural to show. We can do no more than let others judge for themselves what we inwardly and really are, and do the same ourselves with them. The one essential thing is that we strive to have light in ourselves."[2]

He understands not only his own right to privacy, but the difficulty we have of properly comprehending the motives and natures of others. He wrote: "We wander through life together in a semi-darkness in which none of us can distinguish exactly the features of his neighbor; only from time to time, through some experience that we have of our companion, or through some remark that he passes, he stands for a moment close to us, as though illumined by a flash of lightning. Then we see him as he really is."[3]

These passages from his earlier writings have undoubtedly recurred to him as he has read the misinformation and disdainful challenges made of his life's effort. His daughter, Mrs. Rhena Eckert-Schweitzer, said that he was personally hurt by every attack made on the hospital or his ideas, feeling them as though they were personal attacks on him as an individual; yet he suffered them in silence. Unquestionably he did not know the bitterness or extensive nature such attacks would take when he wrote, "I myself have lacked love, have hated, slandered, defrauded, and been arrogant. . . ." These were written in more polite and less critical days, and were a matter of degree, whereas in his final years attacks went to the full extreme. One will search the record and events of Schweitzer's life in vain for evidences of hatred, slander or fraud. The spirit of humility and self-abasement were always an attribute of Schweitzer, however.

1 *Reader's Digest,* Oct. 1949 (Dr. Schweitzer in interview with Fulton Oursler).

2 *Memoirs of Childhood and Youth,* p. 70.

3 *Ibid.,* pp. 68-69.

He once highlighted the steady lowering of human standards in our society when he wrote: "We believed once in the victory of truth; but we do not now. We believed in our fellow-men; but we do not now. We believed in goodness; but we do not now. We were zealous for justice; but we are not so now. We trusted in the power of kindness and peaceableness; we do not now. We were capable of enthusiasm; but we are not so now. To get through the shoals and storms of life more easily we have lightened our craft, throwing overboard what we thought could be spared. But it was really our stock of food and drink of which we deprived ourselves; our craft is now easy to manage, but we ourselves are in decline."[4]

It is in the spirit of this passage that he has written, "With the spirit of the age I am in complete disagreement."[5]

Yet he has held fast to his own counsel and to his own integrity. He wrote on another occasion: "The great secret of success is to go through life as a man who never gets used up. That is possible for him who never argues and strives with men and facts, but in all experience retires upon himself, and looks for the ultimate cause of things in himself."[6]

In spite of the shortcomings of our world and culture, a man by taking counsel of himself, and doing what he knows to be right, can find his way through the labyrinth, and "never get used up." This was part of his secret.

He was a complex man, a man of thought and depth, always stirring controversy, but never participating directly in it, because he stood as an individualist, a dissenter, a non-conformist. He was one of the great free-minded independents who speak and act for themselves, without a thought of what the world expects. He was, indeed, almost unconscious of the world's expectations of him, and so he went his solitary way as the last of the great non-conformists.

In recent years the criticisms have been repeated more frequently concerning his independent and unorthodox views; as the remote jungle receded and modern Africa became a

[4] *Ibid.*, p. 74.
[5] *Out of My Life and Thought*, Epilogue, p. 254.
[6] *Memoirs of Childhood and Youth*, p. 76.

floodlit stage, it was inevitable that Schweitzer would be thrust forward into the spotlight, reluctant though he might be. However, he conducted himself well through the verbal ordeal to which he was subjected. In dignity and with modest acceptance he went silently to his grave.

Yet his voice will not be silenced. His printed word lives on and, more important, the personal influence of his life on others will continue to make its mark. Is it possible, further, that he had found (as he believed) the first, original new ethical concept of mankind—Reverence for Life—and opened the door to a new ethical, philosophical and religious orientation? Many who have studied and known him believe so. On September 12, 1965, *The New York Times,* in its section "The News of the Week in Review," wrote: "When Dr. Albert Schweitzer died this week at his jungle compound in Lambaréné, Gabon, he left behind a typically far-ranging influence on religious life and thought. It extended from a pivotal contribution in the area of New Testament criticism to his role as a symbol of religious piety for Christian liberals." The article also noted that "His attitude towards religion—as opposed to the primarily philosophical idea of 'Reverence for Life'—remains unclear."

According to *The Times,* that attitude on religion will become clarified by the discovery of the missing document it referred to—his proposed posthumous statement on religion left in 1949 with Dr. Frederick May Eliot, who preceded Dr. Schweitzer to the grave. Its whereabouts is unknown at the moment. It will undoubtedly remain for future evaluation rather than present documents to clarify the religious position and role of Albert Schweitzer.

Many have called Schweitzer a saint in our day. Perhaps he was. However, he denied, and angrily rejected, such references. Others have suggested that, like Gandhi, he had the genuine markings of a latter day religious savior, a founder of a new religion. His friends and close associates avoid any such thought, although they are attentive and listen when it is suggested that at a future time the hippopotamus may—like the fish—become a religious symbol, and the palm tree—like the cross—a sign of veneration. His numerous writings, classic in their content and style, as well as original and forward looking in their concepts, may lead to a following long after most other modern names are forgotten. One dare not speculate on this point, and yet there are hints of a rich contribution to religious lore in his life as well as thought.

How many contemporaries expected that Socrates, Jesus, Confucius, Mohammed, or Gautama, would live on and become a focal point for millions? All, like Schweitzer, became controversial characters in their own time, several even to the point of death or exile. All were charismatic personages, and all were recognized as possessing an undeniably spiritual nature in their own lives. All, likewise, had an articulate, loyal, inner following, which they could not dispense with even when they wished. No serious person today forecasts this as happening with Schweitzer. The Doctor would, certainly, have vehemently rejected the entire idea.

Rather, he would ask of his followers simply that they be ethically concerned, more considerate, generous, tolerant, and kindly—and that they not forget that thinking is religious, and that the affirmation of thought is the beginning of wisdom.

Words from his *Memoirs of Childhood and Youth* are perhaps the best benediction to his life:

> Hence I always think that we all live, spiritually, by what others have given us in the significant hours of our life. These significant hours do not announce themselves as coming, but arrive unexpected. Nor do they make a great show of themselves; they pass almost unperceived. Often, indeed their significance comes home to us first as we look back, just as the beauty of a piece of music or of a landscape often strikes us first in our recollection of it. Much that has become our own in gentleness, modesty, kindness, willingness to forgive, in veracity, loyalty, resignation under suffering, we owe to people in whom we have seen or experienced these virtues at work, sometimes in a great matter, sometimes in a small. A thought which had become act sprang into us like a spark, and lighted a new flame within us.

I do not believe that we can put into anyone ideas which are not in him already. As a rule there are in everyone all sorts of good ideas, ready like tinder. But much of this tinder catches fire, or catches it successfully, only when it meets some flame or spark from outside, i.e. from some other person. Often, too, our own light goes out, and is rekindled by some experience we go through with a fellow-man. Thus we have each of us cause to think with deep gratitude of those who have lighted the flames within us.

APPENDIX A

Lambaréné, September 8, 1965

Association de l'Hôpital du
Dr. Albert Schweitzer
Lambaréné / Gabon.
Siege Social Strasbourg / France
President Dr. Fritz Schnepp
9*a, Rue de Geneve, Strasbourg.*

To the Board of Directors of
the Committees for The Albert
Schweitzer Hospital in Lambaréné.

Dear Friends,

After the passing of our dear Albert Schweitzer the Association of Strasbourg has become in effect the proprietor of the Albert Schweitzer Hospital in Lambaréné, as it was foreseen in our statutes since 1931/33 and has been put down in the legal act of October 13, 1933.

In a letter of July 1964 Dr. Schweitzer has designated Walter Munz M.D. from Arbon, Switzerland, as the doctor in charge of his hospital in Lambaréné. Dr. Munz has been carrying on this function since February 1965.

In a letter which he has written to our Association on August 23, 1965, Dr. Schweitzer declares that it is his wish that his daughter Rhena Eckert-Schweitzer, actually staying in Lambaréné, take over the direction of his hospital after his death.

So to avoid a break in the direction and the continuation of the work in the Lambaréné hospital the members of the Strasbourg Association, who are present in Lambaréné (Mme. Emmy Martin, Mlle. Mathilde Kottmann, M. Charles Michel) have agreed that, according to the wishes of Dr. Schweitzer, Rhena Eckert-Schweitzer and Dr. Walter Munz take over the responsibility for the continuation of the work in the hospital in the spirit of its founder. A formal consent of all the members of the Association will be asked in a general meeting to be held in Strasbourg as soon as possible.

This meeting will also have to deal with the problems concerning the future of the Lambaréné Hospital, especially and most urgently with the organization of an international meeting. The results of the decisions will be made known with all the details to the committees of the different countries.

We are convinced that if it had been possible for Dr. Schweitzer, he would have informed personally all the committees of his last will. As, unfortunately, fate did not give him time to do so, we have taken it upon ourselves to let it be known to you as soon as possible.

In deep grief, but with the confident hope that the work which is dear to the heart of all of us will continue with your help as a living monument to the memory of our dear and revered Grand Docteur.

With cordial regards,

M. Charles Michel
Mme. Emmy Martin
Mlle. Mathilde Kottmann

APPENDIX B

Lambaréné, 20th September 1965

REPORT ABOUT THE MEETING OF MRS. RHENA ECKERT-SCHWEITZER, DR. WALTER MUNZ AND MR. CHARLES MICHEL OF STRASBOURG WITH PRESIDENT LEON MBA OF THE REPUBLIC OF GABON, AFRICA.

After the death of Doctor Albert Schweitzer it seemed right and necessary to contact the President of the Republic of Gabon, His Excellence Leon MBa, the Vice-President, and several other Representatives of the Government in Libreville, to speak about the hopes and wishes of Doctor Albert Schweitzer regarding the future of the hospital he founded in 1913.

Mrs. Rhena Eckert-Schweitzer, Doctor Walter Munz and Mr. Charles Michel of Strasbourg asked for a meeting with the head of the Republic of Gabon. Answer came immediately through the Praefect of Lambaréné that the President would be happy to receive us. The meeting was arranged for September 15th at 10 o'clock in the forenoon.

Mr. Nboudy, the Chief of Protocol, received us very cordially. He, a pupil of the former mission school of Bongolo, had himself been a patient of the Albert Schweitzer Hospital when he was a boy.

At 10:20 we were asked to meet the President in his study. He welcomed us with great warmth and simplicity. He received us without entourage, alone and informally.

The President immediately expressed his deeply felt sympathy and explained how sad he was to have been absent during the funeral ceremonies, but on account of the recent death of his own father, he was compelled, according to African custom, to remain secluded, inside of his dwelling, for three months.

Mrs. Rhena Eckert-Schweitzer thanked the President in her own name, as well as that of the Association in Strasbourg and all others and foundations which throughout the world help the Schweitzer Hospital, for the President and his Government's sharing of their grief.

Then, Mrs. Eckert-Schweitzer informed the President of her father's decided wish that the Albert Schweitzer Hospital should continue. She assured the President that those whom her father had charged with the great responsibility of running the hospital from now on have accepted this duty as a sacred heritage to do their utmost to fulfill this task in the spirit of her father.

She then expressed her hope that the President would continue his friendship and grant moral support as he had always done during her father's life time.

Dr. Walter Munz, expressing the identical wish, added that besides the continuance of the hospital it was planned to employ medical progress, extension of their program of preventive medicine, hygiene installations, water supply and canalization, in the near future, so that the patients at the Albert Schweitzer Hospital would be assured the most beneficial treatment.

Mr. Charles Michel assured President Leon MBa that the Association of the Albert Schweitzer Hospital in Strasbourg in conjunction with all the other aid foundations throughout the world have pledged their continued help so that the Albert Schweitzer Hospital, founded in 1913 and run for over 52 years, could not only remain open to help all those who came for medical treatment but enlarge its activities in step with modern times.

The President answered first by speaking with deep emotion of the passing of his old friend. He spoke of the loss to his country and praised the selfless work Dr. Schweitzer had given to his countrymen. He encouraged us to do all we can to continue the work of the hospital and promised his personal help and that of his co-workers, whenever needed.

He especially asked not to tear down the old buildings, but to keep the village atmosphere which made everyone feel at home, even if confined to a hospital. This, he remarked, had shown Dr. Schweitzer's complete understanding and compassion for his people and it was for those the Doctor had sacrificed his strength. The improvements should be done in le Grand Docteur's spirit and fit into this frame of mind.

The Gabon, the President continued, is proud of this great adopted son; it is his own personal desire that the Hospital Albert Schweitzer remain a living monument of true, active Christianity, established by his admired and beloved friend, the late Dr. Albert Schweitzer.

In simple and convincing words the President assured us also of his complete support regarding unforeseen problems which might arise in the future. All of us thanked him for his recognition of Dr. Schweitzer's work and for his words of encouragement to continue the Hospital in Lambaréné on which the eyes of the world rest as a center of hope and humanity.

The visits to the Gabonese Vice President, Mr. Yembit and the Minister for Water and Forestry, Mr. Avaro, showed us the same warm cordiality and we realized gratefully that the lifelong work of Dr. Albert Schweitzer on the Ogowe River has not only left its mark in the hearts of his patients and the other people of the Gabon, but also in the circles of Government.

M. Charles Michel
Dr. Walter Munz
Mrs. Rhena Eckert-Schweitzer

BIBLIOGRAPHY

Albert Schweitzer, *African Notebook,* New York, Holt, 1939.

Albert Schweitzer, *Indian Thought and Its Development,* Boston, Beacon Paperback ed., 1960; *Goethe: Five Studies,* Charles Joy, Ed., Beacon Paperback ed., 1961.

Albert Schweitzer, *Memoirs of Childhood and Youth,* New York, Macmillan Paperback ed., 1963.

Albert Schweitzer, *On the Edge of the Primeval Forest* and *More from the Primeval Forest,* New York, Macmillan, 1931 (reissued 1961).

Albert Schweitzer, *Out of My Life and Thought,* New York, Henry Holt Co., 1933. This is the edition referred to above and quoted in text and footnotes.

Albert Schweitzer, *Out of My Life and Thought,* New York, Holt, 1949, with a "Postscript 1923-49" by Everett Skillings. This work is cited as 1949 ed. in footnotes.

Albert Schweitzer, *Peace or Atomic War?,* New York, Holt, Rinehart & Winston.

Albert Schweitzer, *The Philosophy of Civilization,* Part I: *The Decay and Restoration of Civilization;* Part II: *Civilization and Ethics,* New York, Macmillan Paperback ed., 1960.

Albert Schweitzer, *The Quest of the Historical Jesus,* New York, Macmillan, 1961.

Charles Joy, Ed., *Albert Schweitzer: An Anthology,* New York, Harper, 1947; Enlarged edition, Boston, Beacon Paperback ed., 1955.

Albert Schweitzer, *Pilgrimage to Humanity,* New York, Philosophical Library, 1961.

Erica Anderson and Eugene Exman, *The World of Albert Schweitzer,* New York, Harper, 1955.

Albert Schweitzer, *Reverence for Life,* Thomas Kiernan, Ed., New York, Philosophical Library, 1965.

L. Ostergaard-Christensen, *At Work With Albert Schweitzer,* Boston, Beacon, 1962.

Norman Cousins (with Clara Urquhart), *Dr. Schweitzer of Lambaréné,* New York, Harper & Row, 1960.
Charles Joy and Melvin Arnold, *The Africa of Albert Schweitzer,* New York, Harper, 1948; Boston, Beacon, 1948.
Gabriel Langfeldt, *Albert Schweitzer, A Study of His Philosophy of Life,* New York, Braziller, 1960.
Magnus Ratter, *Albert Schweitzer, Life and Message,* Boston, Beacon, 1950.
George Seaver, *Albert Schweitzer, A Vindication,* Boston, Beacon, 1951.
George Seaver, *Albert Schweitzer, Christian Revolutionary,* New York, Harper, 1944; *Albert Schweitzer, The Man and His Mind,* Harper, 1947.
John Gunther, *Inside Africa,* New York, Harper; Chapter 35, "A Visit to Dr. Albert Schweitzer."
Gerald McKnight, *Verdict on Schweitzer,* New York, John Day, 1964.
Erica Anderson, *Albert Schweitzer's Gift for Friendship,* New York, Harper & Row, 1964; *The Albert Schweitzer Album,* also Harper & Row, 1965.
Werner Picht, *The Life and Thought of Albert Schweitzer,* New York, Harper & Row, 1965.
Henry Clark, *Ethical Mysticism of Albert Schweitzer,* Boston, Beacon Press, 1962.

Acknowledgments

The author is grateful for permission to quote from the following:

Inside Africa by John Gunther, by permission of Harper & Row, Inc., New York; *Dr. Schweitzer of Lambarene* by Norman Cousins, by permission of Harper & Row, Inc., New York; *Out of my Life and Thought* by Albert Schweitzer, translated by C. T. Campion, copyright 1933, 1949 by Holt, Rinehart & Winston, Inc., reprinted by permission of Holt, Rinehart & Winston, Inc., New York; *Peace or Atomic War?* by Albert Schweitzer, reprinted by permission of Holt, Rinehart & Winston, Inc., New York; *Philosophy of Civilization* by Albert Schweitzer, reprinted by permission of The Macmillan Company, New York; *Memoirs of Childhood and Youth* by Albert Schweitzer, reprinted by permission of The Macmillan Company, New York; *On the Edge of the Primeval Forest* by Albert Schweitzer, by permission of The Macmillan Company, New York; *Quest of the Historical Jesus* by Albert Schweitzer, reprinted by permission of The Macmillan Company, New York; *The Verdict on Schweitzer* by Conor Cruise O'Brien, reprinted from The New York Review of Books, copyright 1964, The New York Review; *The Verdict on Schweitzer* by Card D. Howard, by permission of The National Observer; *The Doctor Darkly* by John Gunther, courtesy The New York Times; *Words to Live By* from *Discover Your True Worth* by Bernard S. Redmont, reprinted from This Week Magazine, copyright 1959 by the United Newspaper Magazine Corporation; *The Press's Myth of Dr. Schweitzer* by Russell Howe, courtesy The Washington Post; *The Fall of Schweitzer* by William Buckley, courtesy Washington Star Syndicate, Inc.